Contributions to Management Science

The series *Contributions to Management Science* contains research publications in all fields of business and management science. These publications are primarily monographs and multiple author works containing new research results, and also feature selected conference-based publications are also considered. The focus of the series lies in presenting the development of latest theoretical and empirical research across different viewpoints.

This book series is indexed in Scopus.

Peter Droege • Stefan Güldenberg
Marco J. Menichetti • Stefan Seidel
Editors

Cross-Border Life and Work

Social, Economic, Technological and Jurisdictional Issues

Springer

Editors
Peter Droege
Liechtenstein Institute for Strategic Development AG
Vaduz, Liechtenstein

Marco J. Menichetti
Liechtenstein Business School
University of Liechtenstein
Vaduz, Liechtenstein

Stefan Güldenberg
EHL Hospitality Business School, HES-SO
Lausanne, Switzerland

Stefan Seidel
University of Cologne
Cologne, Germany

ISSN 1431-1941 ISSN 2197-716X (electronic)
Contributions to Management Science
ISBN 978-3-031-34361-2 ISBN 978-3-031-34362-9 (eBook)
https://doi.org/10.1007/978-3-031-34362-9

This Springer imprint is published by the registered company Springer Nature Switzerland AG
The registered company address is: Gewerbestrasse 11, 6330 Cham, Switzerland

Preface

This book presents results from an interdisciplinary research project on cross-border life and work. The project, born of cross faculty collaborations at the University of Liechtenstein, was motivated by the specific regional circumstances found in the Alpine Rhine Valley—a cross-border region that belongs to different national states but also has its own distinct cultural identity. Here key institutions—communities, governments, corporations, and markets—face challenges and risks but also powerful opportunities due to the enriching social, political, economic, environmental, historical and jurisdictional differences.

In this cross-border and interdisciplinary volume, we address some of the most pertinent issues in this context. In the chapter "Regional Affordances and Resilient Communities," Anis Radzi, Peter Droege, Stefan Seidel, Barbara Fuchs, and Marco Menichetti set the scene by describing the concept of *regional affordances*—the actionable spaces that emerge as relationships between the available physical and informational support structures and the communities that act upon those support structures. They specifically focus attention on how such regional affordances provide action potentials required for sustainability and resilience. In the chapter "Site Selection According to Life Cycles in Agglomeration Areas: A Dynamic and Interdisciplinary Location Analysis of the Four-Country-Region Lake Constance-Alpine Rhine Valley," Stefan Güldenberg, Laura Hecker, Adrian Klammer, Francesco Schurr, Peter Staub, and Stefan Wilhelm summarize findings from an empirical study on the differences and similarities that arise in polycentric border-crossing agglomerations. They identify factors that influence the residential choice in such regions in a knowledge-based economy. In the chapter "Cross-Border Philanthropy: Current Challenges in Corporate Governance and Financial Risk Management," Francesco Schurr and Marco Menichetti describe why Liechtenstein is an ideal hub for local and international philanthropic foundations. They analyze how law-making in Liechtenstein supports international philanthropic projects. Next, in "Cross-Border Wealth Management," Martin Angerer, Michael Hanke, Tanja Kirn, Christina Preiner, Martin Wenz, Dirk Zetzsche, and Michael Amann analyze the economic, legal, and tax-related drivers and barriers to cross-border wealth management. They complement their analysis with a discussion of related global developments. In "Crowdfunding in German-Speaking Countries: A Literature Review from an Economics and Legal Perspective," Martin Angerer, Sascha Kraus, and Andreas Peter identify three key success factors relevant to cross-border investors in crowdfunding related to behavioral biases, multiple taxation systems, and multiple legislation. Finally, in "Family Business across National Borders: Strategies and Processes of Internationalization," Philipp Stieg, Sascha Kraus, Tanja Kirn, and Marco Menichetti discuss strategies and processes for internationalization of family businesses across borders. Specifically, they focus on a financial perspective.

Together, these chapters provide insights into the multifarious issues related to cross-border life and work. We take into consideration the diverse and multilayered social, economic, technological, and jurisdictional issues of cross-border regions, and we explore some of the risks, challenges, and opportunities of cross-border work and life from an interdisciplinary perspective. The challenges of this cross-border situation became accentuated with the global pandemic of 2020-22. Physically crossing borders, a key daily practice in a cross-border region, became difficult from one day to another. Organizations had to quickly implement new business practices that would help them overcome those rediscovered borders. Digital infrastructures and technologies provided key resources to overcome spatial barriers and served as shock-absorbers that allowed for organizational resilience. Organizations soon settled on a new normal.

Given this salient cross-border focus, we were also delighted to complete this work in the 50th anniversary year of the International Lake Constance Conference, celebrating a great European cross-border institution and its new intergovernmental commission of four national jurisdictions, cooperatively guiding this metropolitan border region of nearly 15,000 square kilometers and more than four million inhabitants.

Special thanks to Katharina Drechsler and Riley Corbett for their wonderful help with finalizing this manuscript and preparing the final copy. Finally, we thank the University of Liechtenstein Research Fund (FFF) for funding this project (intdis-1-14).

Vaduz, Liechtenstein — Peter Droege
Lausanne, Switzerland — Stefan Güldenberg
Vaduz, Liechtenstein — Marco J. Menichetti
Cologne, Germany — Stefan Seidel
February 2024

Contents

Regional Affordances and Resilient Communities

Anis Radzi, Peter Droege, Stefan Seidel, Barbara Fuchs, and Marco J. Menichetti

Abstract In this chapter, we discuss how regionally available resources - natural, social, economic, and technological - provide regional affordances for individual and collective action and how these are implicated in creating resilient and sustainable communities. We identify regional affordances in terms of learning and innovation, regional coordination, regional measurement and control, regional energetic resilience, regional economic resilience, and regional sustainable finance. We highlight how divergent norms, values, and practices associated with different institutions, including those governing production, social reproduction, and consumption, can conflict with sustainable development and regional resilience.

1 Introduction

Regions are socioeconomic spaces characterized by institutions: social structures comprising of symbolic elements, social activities, and material resources (Scott 2013). Regions are pivotal to the analysis of sustainable development and resilience

A. Radzi
GCGC, Berlin, Germany
e-mail: aradzi@renu.org

P. Droege (✉)
Liechtenstein Institute for Strategic Development AG, Vaduz, Liechtenstein
e-mail: droege@eurisd.org

S. Seidel
University of Cologne, Cologne, Germany
e-mail: stefan.seidel@wiso.uni-koeln.de

B. Fuchs
valma.li, Eschen, Liechtenstein
e-mail: barbara.fuchs@valma.li

M. J. Menichetti
Liechtenstein Business School, University of Liechtenstein, Vaduz, Liechtenstein
e-mail: marco.menichetti@uni.li

P. Droege et al. (eds.), *Cross-Border Life and Work*, Contributions to Management Science, https://doi.org/10.1007/978-3-031-34362-9_1

because their inhabitants are important social, economic, and ecological change agents. As long as there is no apparent and dramatic shock to their institutional systems or social organization, human beings tend to act habitually without questioning future consequences of their behavior. However, current institutional systems have led to rapid degradation of the natural environment and other social and economic threats, and individuals, organizations, and governments are becoming aware of the rising social and ecological cost of current modes of production.

In this chapter, we highlight how *resilience*—a system's ability to return to a stable state after an external shock—is a direct outcome of sustainability: environmental, economic, and social. Here local communities, regions, and nations have long been compelled by international frameworks, such as the Paris Agreement under the United Nations Framework Convention on Climate Change (UNFCCC) and the United Nations Sustainable Development Goals (UN SDGs). The Paris Climate Agreement of October 5, 2016, signed by the vast majority of parties (UNFCC 2016), has added a considerable momentum to this push, as have the Sustainable Development Goals (SDGs)—officially named Transforming our World: The 2030 Agenda for Sustainable Development—adopted on September 25, 2015 (United Nations 2016).

Considerable challenges to sustainable practice for resilient regions exist, and this chapter is a reasoned call to overcome these. Existing institutions including those governing consumption, production, and social reproduction can be at conflict with sustainable development and regional resilience. Current modes of production and distribution tend to have neglected increasing social and ecological cost, materializing, for instance, in the form of climate destabilization, species extinctions, competition for natural resources, declining ecological services, unemployment, and poverty.

Communities aiming at resilience as one of the most important conditions and outcomes of sustainable development have thus to consider the quality and mechanisms of their institutions, to strengthen those institutions that support resilience, and to initiate change where needed. In the case of regional communities spanning across the borders of adjoining nation states, it is even more important to consider and challenge the institutional framework from the perspectives of resilience and sustainability. The formulation of cross-border common goals and the design of common and collective actions are important challenges requiring the consideration of the institutional arrangements and roles of different nation states simultaneously.

Against this background, we draw on institutional theory as well as the concept of affordance known from the field of ecological psychology to develop a theoretical framework that accounts for (1) the institutional context of sustainable resource use and regional resilience and (2) potential action spaces to secure and increase resilience within such institutional context. We use the notion of *regional affordance* to allow for the identification of various action potentials offered by natural, economic, social, and technological resources—i.e., by material and social structures—for the pursuit of regional resilience. Regions provide affordances in the sense of possibilities for goal-oriented action to their members.

We specifically focus on those affordances that are created in cross-border regions. While previous studies have mainly focused their attention on sustainable development and resilience in a regional context, little attention has been paid to the cross-border regions that can touch the institutional architecture of different nation states. It is expected that understanding how affordances of cross-border regions can be created based on different resource configurations and institutional contexts will provide insights into how programs can be developed to establish resilient communities at the level of policy formulation as well as decision-making.

We proceed as follows. First, we describe the concept of resilient regions. Second, we outline the concept of regional affordances. We then discuss some regional affordances that can help address key challenges to regional resilience in terms of regional learning and innovation, regional coordination, regional measurement and control, regional energetic resilience, regional economic resilience, and regional sustainable financing. At this, we highlight how tensions may exist, which regional actors must overcome—such as between the regional context and the national/international context as well as because of the potential cross-border nature of regions. We then provide a conceptual framework of regional affordances as an analytical device to study regional resilience and sustainability and provide some concluding remarks.

2 Resilient Regions

2.1 Resilience

The concept of resilience is closely related to the capability of an element or a system to return to a stable state after an external shock, for example, natural disasters, or some form of disruption arising from the system itself, such as the advent of disruptive technologies. Resilience denotes both the speed of return to equilibrium following perturbations and the size of a disturbance needed to remove a system from its stability domain (Holling 1973). The latter may be interpreted as the probability that a system residing in a specific stability domain will flip into another stability domain given its current state as well as the disturbance regime (Perrings 1998). A resilient system can be characterized by low failure probability and reduced failure consequences, which corresponds to a basic static definition of resilience, and short recovery time, which adds a temporal dynamic dimension to the basic definition (Rose 2007).

Researchers have related the concept of resilience to the concept of sustainability, i.e., to long-term survival and a nondecreasing quality of life (Common 1995; Perrings 2001). Furthermore, *adaptive resilience*, or perhaps better *dynamic resilience*, enables the combined ecological, social, and economic system to adapt itself in response to shocks with the possibility to renew its own structures on a sustainable development path.

In resilient societies, citizens possess the intellectual and emotional capability and capacity to anticipate, react, and transform system structures, both material and social, in response to shocks and disturbances (Bristow and Healy 2014). People are active agents in resilience, defined as a set of capabilities and competences that can be developed and acquired through the accumulation of knowledge and the social interaction of community members in a spatial context (Magis 2010). In this socio-economic context, resilience also bears a normative meaning. A shared vision must exist within the (regional) community about what the normal stable state of the common system is, what potential strategies are to react to disturbances to maintain that desired state, and in which ways the system must be renewed to reach the next desirable stable state on a long-term sustainable development path. Resilience is then a concept that is closely linked to institutions that have developed over time and resulting from human agency nested in the bounded spatial context that is often referred to as a region. The resilience of a region is largely influenced by the opportunities and constraints offered by the natural environment, the accumulation of knowledge, the transformation of that knowledge into social practices, and a shared system of norms and beliefs that shapes human interactions.

2.2 Regions

Regions are geographically and historically contingent spaces that are constructed and experienced through shared social practices spanning across the, often artificial, borders of nation states. They are bounded geographical spaces that have similar kinds of land, water, fauna, and flora and that are inhabited by people sharing some important cultural features such as language or religious beliefs. They provide shelter, affinity, sustenance, and webs of linkages. They are at once spatial surfaces, natural ecologies, webs of infrastructure, economic marketplaces, and sociocultural interfaces that carry profound existential significance and meaning. They do so by virtue of the social articulation and cultural interpretation of the ecological and economic resource base underlying them.

The identification of a region is highly dependent on the specific question of investigation since the region as an identifiable unit arises primarily from the individual perspective of the viewer (Wiechmann 2000). In relational terms, regions can simply be distinguished physically as coherent partial spaces of medium size in a larger domain that is characterized or defined by certain traits (Akademie für Raumforschung und Landesplanung (Hg) 1994). Alternatively, a region can be seen as merely a manifestation of society's search for authentic units of an intermediate scale based on analyses of areas that have either a homogenous structure or functional linkages (Wiechmann 2000). As "an area of activity or thought, a region is really a consequence of political will, in that it does not exist in itself but rather represented as a designed unit" (Boesch 1989, p. 68). It is important to augment this spatially grounded understanding with the appurtenant geographically, climatically, regio-economically, demographically, historically, or culturally defined dimensions that make regions work as regions.

2.3 The Argument for Resilience: Regional Risk Management

To understand what a region can afford in relation to rendering it resilient, we must first understand the argument for resilience, which brings us to a discussion of *risk*. The insurance industry—as well as the Intergovernmental Panel on Climate Change (IPCC)—refers to risk as being assessed by understanding specific hazards and one's exposure to them. Resilience relates to an ecological, economic, or social system's ability to adapt to and cope with these risks, generally subscribing to the following formula: risk = hazard x exposure/resilience (or systemic capacity to adapt to hazard x exposure, socially, economically, institutionally, and ecologically). Resilience management means both counteracting the root causes of man-made hazards and adapting to their unavoidable effects.

The topic has been much debated and long been associated with environmental studies and planning, with psychology and other social sciences, in relation to natural disaster management and regional climate adaptation as well as mitigation. Today, a general feeling of uncertainty and insecurity has kept the focus squarely on this topic. This need for resilience has now become a response to an "increased sense of risk (economic and political as well as environmental), and from the perception that processes associated with globalization have made places and regions more permeable to the effects of what were once thought to be external processes" (Christopherson et al. 2010, p. 3).

There is a sense that regions—and their communities—have become more and more exposed to global events and subsequent effects over the past decades: oil crises, nuclear power accidents, regional power outages, world economic crises, global terrorism, climate change impacts, and, among these, more recently, the global refugee crises as well as the COVID pandemic. These disturbances have occurred as abrupt and distinct events or have evolved gradually as recurring or slowly intensifying challenges (Pendall et al. 2010). As these emergencies intersect, the sense of vulnerability is heightened. How can regions respond to such risks? How can they go beyond merely adapting to economic, environmental, and social disruptions but also avoid, militate against, prepare for, and respond positively to future disturbances?

The concept of *regional affordance* can help us understand the action potentials provided by regions to respond to risks and crises and to thus enact appropriate responses to such disturbances. The key point is that there is no deterministic way to mitigate risk in complex adaptive systems such as regions. Instead, regional actors as change agents must perceive and actively shape the actionable spaces that regional resources as well as the institutional context provide for actions that can help decrease failure probability, reduce consequence from failure, and allow for short time of recovery.

Resilient communities will need to become self-sufficient in resources, be self-aware, and develop a sense of purpose. They will manifest themselves as, for instance, (a) energy autonomous municipalities or regions, (b) transition towns, (c) selected green communities, and (d) urban communities of the prosumer or prosumption movement. The prosumption community, in particular, will integrate distributed information management and communications and the rise of distributed renewable energy generation in order to increase local and regional self-reliance, prosperity, regional monetary gain, atmospheric carbon uptake, and innovational impulses that transcend regional boundaries (Droege 2014).

3 Regional Affordances and Constraints

We adopt the concept of affordance, originally proposed in the field of ecological psychology to describe the relationships between animals and the environment (Gibson 1977), to refer to the potential actions that regions provide to communities. Note that we are applying the concept at the level of actor groups, that is, regional actors representing key institutional orders such as state, market, and corporation. In this view, regional affordances describe the relationships between the available physical and informational support structures and the communities that act upon those support structures:

> An important fact about the affordances of the environment is that they are in a sense objective, real, and physical, unlike values and meanings, which are often supposed to be subjective, phenomenal, and mental. But, actually, an affordance is neither an objective property nor a subjective property; or it is both if you like. An affordance cuts across the dichotomy of subjective-objective and helps us to understand its inadequacy. It is equally a fact of the environment and a fact of behaviour. It is both physical and psychical, yet neither. (Gibson 1979, p. 129)

Expanding Gibson's original concept to human beings—and groups of human beings—affordances describe opportunities offered by the natural and artificial surroundings to their inhabitants, that is, in terms of material and social structures. For instance, fertile grounds and water afford agricultural practices. At the same time, affordances refer to the institutional aspect of system structures and norms that determine the likelihood of humans to act upon these opportunities, the ways in which they act, and how their individual and collective action will affect regional resilience and sustainable development.

Resilience and sustainable development paths are strongly linked through the creation, use, development, and specific application of technical objects and systems. Digital technology, for example, can be used to strengthen regional resilience (as the COVID pandemic has shown) but can also constrain and erode regional systems. The concept of affordances thus helps describe and analyze action potentials within a spatially contingent socioeconomic system and its material and social structures to enable decision-making and to formulate policies and strategies for renewal that follow a sustainable development path and thus foster resilience.

Against this backdrop, *we define regional affordances as the action potentials provided by the available natural, constructed, and informational support structures to the regional communities that interact with those support structures.* They are thus relations between material and social structures and regional actors that describe action potentials that, if enacted, lead to practices supporting regional resilience. Next, we illustrate how material and social structures afford regional resilience.

Natural resources traditionally afforded humankind specific opportunities for survival and prosperity, such as hunting and building, and at the same time defined and even constrained human action. The natural habitat has a strong influence on the accumulation of local knowledge and how humans make use of their knowledge base to sustain life in material ways and to create specific stocks of knowledge for their own well-being (Berkes 1999). Within the natural space of living, knowledge is based on observations and experience that humans have acquired through their contact with the local environment. Language, too, can be understood as a "resource for nature" (Maffi 1998), and "any reduction of language diversity diminishes the adaptive strength of our species because it lowers the pool of knowledge from which we can draw" (Bernard 1992, p. 82). Regions defined as socially constructed spatial contexts also have a strong influence on the construction and experience of home and feelings of being at home because individuals and groups project themselves on a specific spatial and social territory (Terkenli 1995).

In many regions, public authorities and private economic agents invest in public facilities and commercial or residential buildings in the hope of attracting social life and economic activity to a specific place. Let us suppose that the buildings are designed and built following principles of sustainability such as the use of renewable materials and energy. The buildings as technical objects introduce inhabitants of the region to the opportunity to purchase or rent a shop for their own entrepreneurial activities or to consume whatever other tenants of the buildings offer. Still, does the mere provision of material infrastructure indeed lead to the intended response? In applying the concept of affordances, we can argue that human action does not deterministically result from the mere provision of new infrastructure but can only be explained by both simple and complex systems of recognizing, valuing, identifying, and enacting possibilities provided by that infrastructure, in consideration of other factors shaping individual and collective behavior. In our example, an analysis of both complementary and competing affordances, with respect to regional resilience and sustainability, might shed light on whether the intentions of the builder are likely to be indeed fulfilled (or, e.g., are in sharp contrast with the affordances the empty space offers to inhabitants) and in which ways the infrastructure has to be complemented with other affordances, such as for superior transport infrastructure, education, entertainment, or recreational opportunities.

While in the literature a broad discussion exists about the determinants of regional resilience (e.g., Bristow and Healy 2014; Martin and Sunley 2015), we suggest that the concept of affordances might enrich our understanding of resilience in a number of ways. Next, we discuss some important challenges related to the resilience of regions as well as affordances that help regions respond to those challenges.

4 Evolutionary Regional Resilience

Every region is susceptible to risks—localized or global pressures that impact the efficacy and success of material and social support structures and the relationship of regional actors with those structures. A risk being "the possibility of loss, injury, or other adverse or unwelcome circumstance; a chance or situation involving such a possibility" (Oxford English Dictionary 2010a, b) will require measures that temper, counteract, and adapt to those facing it. The insurance industry, for example—in a nuanced modification of the IPCC's frames (IPCC 2022)—defines risk in the context of climate change vulnerability as a function of hazard, exposure, and natural as well as societal resilience (Crichton et al. 2009). This takes on special meaning in the context of regional climate change adaptation and mitigation, or mitaptation (Droege 2006).

A region therefore must be sufficiently robust to be able to quickly overcome and recover from societal, economic, and environmental pressures over time. It must be resilient, that is, being elastic to such pressures, while also possessing the "quality or fact of being able to recover quickly or easily from, or resist being affected by, a misfortune, shock, illness, etc." (Oxford English Dictionary). However, to gauge the degree of resilience or robustness will depend on the identification of the regional affordances as well as constraints. While affordances are the action potentials provided, constraints (such as limited resource availability) may also exist. In this chapter, our key focus is on the affordances and how regional communities can discover, enact, and actively shape these affordances.

Next, we describe categories of interrelated regional affordances for resilient regional practices. By no means do we mean to be exhaustive. Instead, we aim to highlight how regions—grounded in their natural and designed elements in terms of material and social structures—afford actors resilient behavior and how these actionable spaces may evolve as human agencies, institutions (social structures), and physical and informational infrastructures (material structures) change over time. In this view, regional affordances are no stable discrete elements, but they are evolving relational, actionable spaces that change as human agencies, institutions, and material structures evolve. Change and evolution are the very essence of urban development and regional planning. Towns, cities, and regions continuously adapt, react, and grow into physical entities that fit their emerging cultures, economies, and ecologies. They undergo dynamic and fluctuating processes that result in the expansion or contraction of their natural and built environments. As change is inevitable, for regions to rebound to their previous states after undergoing a disruption is highly improbable. Resilient regions are not bound to achieve a particular state but rather are open to alternative growth paths by being subjected to deliberate procedures of transformation toward ever greater self-sufficiency.

Here we move beyond the traditional views of resilience: the capacity (a) to respond to change or disturbance without changing its basic state (Walker et al. 2006); or (b) to encompass the processes of rebound, adaptation, and recovery (Hassink 2010); or (c) to shift from one state to "multiple equilibria" (Reggiani et al. 2002; Zolli and Healy 2012). Instead, we opt for the concept of *evolutionary regional resilience*. This approach allows for the consideration of the impacts of human agencies, resources, and institutions over time. It provides different options for growth, optimally selected according to both how effective the path would positively react to immediate short-term shocks and how it can maintain sustainable development practices through effective governance in order to combat long-term challenges (Christopherson et al. 2010; Cooke et al. 2011). This approach enables more flexible, dynamic processes that react to urban and regional contexts, achievable through collective reorganization and repositioning over time in the face of future internal and external disruptions.

Regional Learning and Innovation

Strategies to achieve regional resilience have varied in scale but demonstrate rather similar attitudes around the world. For example, the focus on regional innovation and learning, the resiliency and sustainability of regional infrastructures (energy, water, transport), the development of regional financial support structures, and the steady support of regional economic diversification all acknowledge that a region's capacity to learn, strategize, and regroup is critical. This learning not only refers to the embrace of conceptual and technological advances but also the consideration of inherited social, economic, and environmental circumstances, which help to determine the extent of future intervention.

The operationalization of regional resilience also relies on the level of institutional, industrial, and civic involvement, engagement, and learning, achievable through collaborative processes to plan and implement change (Wolfe 2010) as exemplified in the Transition Town Movement (Hudson 2010).

Not only innovation and learning but also the actual implementation of practices for regional resilience requires coordination, which is a challenge for many regions due to their intermediate level nature. We turn to this aspect next.

Regional Coordination

Coordination refers to the organization of work to allow multiple actors to act collectively toward some common goal. Today, however, regional spatial and infrastructural planning, which often occur across borders, suffer from a lack of coordination and specificity in terms of resource-oriented goals between the many institutions that govern them. Across regions, multiple levels of government operate simultaneously, at transnational, national, state or province, and local levels. Planning policies are generally complementary and supportive between governmental levels within one nation but can differ greatly when compared with those in neighboring countries. These differences usually relate to target-setting, implementation protocols, and policy prioritization. Frequent changes to public policies as a direct response to economic upheavals and election cycles add to the complexity. In Europe, nonbinding and expirable upper-level policies by the European Union (EU) and/or by individual national governments, such as changes in the feed-in tariff or energy policy targets—usually strong proponents of the renewable energy transition—furthermore induce uncertainty and subsequently reluctance by regional villages, towns, and cities to adopt the energy transition. On the other hand, local government incentives on energy efficiency and renewable energy do restore some confidence, supported by the growing presence of nongovernmental agencies willing to assist communities in achieving a level of energetic resilience, for example, the 100% renewable energy towns and regions or 2000-watt society subscribers.

Resilience is not a generally formalized goal for any level of government in Europe at present. Existing spatial planning policies and subsidies are often geared toward mitigating climate change through energetic resilience, but these exist as simple measures in affording the siting, financing, designing, implementation, and running of small-scale independent renewable energy systems, in tandem with generic efficiency measures for all buildings. This is standard practice for local and state spatial planning policymaking. In contrast, there is no such policy at the European or even only at the regional transborder level. Transnational (cross-border) level priorities in energy supply and demand in relation to fuel types (usually oil and gas) and disruption provisions dramatically differ and are by and large still modeled on older energy supply models, which, in turn, are based on vested trading and other commercial interests.

As our discussion has highlighted, the provision of coordination affordances, such as for managing regional energy supply and demand, is closely related to regional measurement and control, to which we turn next.

Regional Measurement and Control

Control broadly describes an agent's (or group of agents') influence toward some predefined goal (Beniger 2009). Control relies on informational capabilities, typically supported by digital technologies (Beniger 2009). The move toward resilient regional energy systems, for instance, not only involves physical support structures but also informational support structures based on digital technologies (Watson et al. 2010). Managing supply- and demand-side intermittency due to the transition toward the use of renewable energy requires key actions in terms of managing deferrables (i.e., deferring the operation of devices to match supply and demand), managing rights markets (for trading consumption rights at the level of energy grids), and dynamic pricing (i.e., determining real-time prices for balancing supply and demand) (Watson et al. 2020). To respond to risks associated with energy supply, such as reliance on unsustainable energy sources and low energy efficiency in a context of volatile energy prices, digital infrastructures and technologies thus play a key role in affording more sustainable energy consumption—and associated emissions—based on material elements in terms of flow networks, sensor networks, and sensitized objects (Watson et al. 2010).

One resource accounting tool that transcends administrative boundaries is the measurement of regional carrying capacities (Rees and Wackernagel 1994, 1996). It is useful in that it highlights the need to understand a region's ability to afford its own natural resources. In spatial terms, it means ascertaining the size of productive land needed to sustain a given population indefinitely with minimal environmental impact. Ecological footprinting (EF) takes this concept further by quantifying the carrying capacity as "the total area of productive land and water required continuously to produce all the resources consumed and to assimilate all the wastes produced, by a defined population, where on Earth the land is located" (Rees and Wackernagel 1996, pp. 228–229). Although EF is a static model and can directly account neither for technological or sociological changes nor for the dynamisms taking place within nature or the regional economy, the concept remains a useful indicator to measure the degree that the region can afford itself the natural resources it needs without compromising its environment at any given point in time. A visualization of the ecological footprints of different countries within a region furthermore affords a useful comparison of resource consumption patterns and a determination of the degrees of resilience within a region. However, such regional differences can only be best understood in context of the spatial planning rules that govern the disparate states, instruments which hugely influence whole areas and landscapes. This impacts the overall affordance of a region to govern its own resources.

While coordination and measurement and control are general regional affordances, we have already highlighted how they are important in one of the key goals of regional resilience—regional energetic resilience—to which we turn next.

Regional Energetic Resilience

Since the oil crises during the 1970s, the primary attempt of regions, cities, and nations to build energy resilience has been to promote efficiency, to promote sufficiency, and to diversify energy supply sources into a good energy mix and even to escape the considerable nonrenewable energy risks altogether. Over time, other crises have surfaced, taking place either abruptly (accidental oil disruptions, speculative price spikes, terrorism, natural disaster, severe weather events) or gradually (resource availability and supply maintenance, political conflicts, climate change). In turn, this has led to the need for more strategic, calculated responses to tackling both short- and long-term disruptions. In the context of energy, regional resilience now calls for a dynamic economy which is able to respond to sudden energy-related changes, handle both temporary and permanent effects, and evolve toward a more energy secure configuration—a process, which is defined as the region's *transformability* (Blum and Legey 2012). This means accounting for both the supply and demand aspects within the regional energy system and its impact on the supply chain and across different urban and regional sectors. As a consequence, the new and most promising aim lies in pursuing exclusive reliance on renewable energy and regional regenerative energy autonomy (Droege 2014).

Out-of-date energy infrastructures such as international pipelines or power networks and oligarchic global energy conglomerates will increase the vulnerability of a region to global disruptions. The evolutionary resilience of a region to transform its energy infrastructures to regional affordances of energetic resilience will require knowledge of the challenges likely to be faced, account for the state of the current systems, gauge their capacity to be transformed, and implement measures to effect the changes over a period of time. In urban and regional planning, a high level of awareness of the region's current capacities is most essential in preparing for its future transformation.

Appropriate energy systems for resilient regions must ensure sustainable and renewable energy self-supply close to the point of demand. Spatial planning rules, in particular, will need to define the interdependencies between energy demand and spatial structure. At the regional scale, attention to energy efficiency, renewable energy production and supply, and carbon management must be considered in relation to the density configuration and form of whole settlements, the transformation of land uses, the reorganization of infrastructure networks, and the sensitive alteration of regional landscapes. In nonspatial terms it will demand institutionally driven, yet collaborative, regional policies that promote energy security, from domestic investment in demand reduction or local renewable energy supply advancement to controlling fuel imports across borders (Bridge et al. 2013). It will require the selection of appropriate decentralized models and governance scales.

While energy supply through energy markets, including decisions about the type of energy transformed, is arguably key element in generating sustainable and resilient communities, regions must also consider the broader economic context in which trade takes places. Here a key challenge is that regions are embedded in larger economic systems and questions arise about how regional economies can counteract exogenous risk originating in that context. We turn to this issue of regional economic resilience next.

Regional Economic Resilience

Despite the globalization of trade and finances, regions remain important ecological, social, and economic entities providing means of living and probably the most important reference system for constructing self-identity through everyday human interactions. While internationalization refers to the increasing importance of trade between or among nations, globalization refers to "global economic integration of many formerly national economies into one global economy, mainly by free trade and free capital mobility, but also by easy or uncontrolled migration" (Daly 1999, p. 31).

Holling's (1973) scientific approach to resilience raises the important question of whether one general equilibrium or multiple stable states can be defined. For example, orthodox economic theory assumes a general equilibrium state in which the supply of goods and services equals demand. Economic resilience is fully aligned with the efficient allocation of resources within the analytical framework of market production (Rose 2007). Under conditions of perfect markets, there is in theory a general market equilibrium as the most efficient solution to the problem of resource allocation. In those approaches faithful to this idea, for example, in environmental economic studies, resilience is basically treated as a separate stock of resource that can be added to the stocks of natural capital, man-made capital, and human capital. If framed, guided, constructed, and managed well, local, regional, national, cross-border, and even international settings can afford circular economies to a significant extent.

As all other capital stocks, economic resilience is measured and quantified for the purpose of calculating and pricing its economic value (Briguglio et al. 2009; Prior and Hagmann 2014). Classical economics commonly conceives of humankind as a collective of autonomous rational agents, independent of any individual history embedded in a broader historical or regional context and acting predominantly on the sole rationality of utility maximization. In consequence of these stylized facts about the human being, the social formation of individual preferences and behavior determined rationalities of care are blended out. Nonmarket production processes and unpaid work in the household and other nonmarket institutions, for instance, local sport associations, nonprofit organizations, and cultural organizations that largely contribute to the social provisioning of goods and personal services and individual well-being, are not considered. Such an economic system can be highly resilient but at the same time detrimental as it may overexploit natural resources and deconstruct diversity of natural resources and human capabilities that are essential for survival of humankind.

One important aspect is how financial markets in regional economies provide actionable spaces for sustainable investments, the issue to which we turn next.

Regional Sustainable Investment

Financial markets are pivotal for economic efficiency (Mishkin and Eakins 2016)—they afford efficient economic transactions and resource allocation. They optimize this contribution to efficiency if their capital allocation function works well. Capital allocation ensures that financial resources are allocated to best performing projects, whereas low performing projects will not receive the aspired funding (Cecchetti and Schoenholtz 2011). Geo-regional financial markets describe those markets of continental regions, such as Asia, Europe, Africa, or the Americas, in distinction to global or international financial markets (Gosh and Ariff 2014). At a more local cross-border level, the idea of regional financial markets is still constrained to local and regional shared investment funds or resource development opportunities in agriculture, renewable energy, or real property.

In the last decades, financial markets have been used to finance any profitable activity, as long as legally not prohibited. It took very long to accomplish a change of mindset (Kiernan 2009). With the increasing interest of investors, financial institutions developed screening methods to guarantee that investments follow sustainable standards. These include exclusion/negative screening, best-in-class/positive screening, engagement and voting, sustainability themes, norms-based screening, impact/community investing, and environmental, social, and governance (ESG) integration. All these screening techniques are used to structure socially responsible investments (SRI) for interested investors. Caused by scandals like Enron or WorldCom, financial institutions started to focus on sound corporate governance practices and companies' return and risk profiles as well as on disclosure of extra-financial performance. This facilitated the creation of a framework to evaluate environmental, social, and corporate governance factors for an individual corporation. Specific rating agencies provide ESG ratings for corporations. ESG can then be integrated into the investment process by structuring portfolios with high ESG ratings.

The key to this mechanism is also to provide reliable forms of transparency and accountability, a quality that is increasingly sought in global or geo-regional investment vehicles. In the EU, the Taxonomy of Sustainable Investing was adopted on April 15, 2020, to provide a guide to institutions and investors as to what constitutes sustainable investments. Such frameworks can be fraught and infringed upon by political and industrial interests, as the inclusion of nuclear power and natural gas systems proposed in 2021 has demonstrated, a move widely decried and rejected by many large offshore investment houses as far from European financial ecosystems as the USA. The local, regional, and global climate and environmental predicaments have long been recognized as a sign of dramatic inefficiency and even failure of markets when it comes to pricing and valuing environmental goods and services—climate change having been called the biggest market failure ever seen (Stern 2006).

Financial markets in a cross-border region offer services to investors across the border, in a global context also called offshore services, but in the context of this report and at the very other end of the financial market scale, these also refer to regional financial frameworks, such as cooperative renewable energy investment structures.

Investors searching for sustainable investment opportunities will cross borders if the offer and service is superior on the other side. In the future, cross-border activities could become increasingly important, as the relative volume and growth rates of sustainable investments are very different across countries (for the situation in Europe, see Eurosif). On the other hand, localization and coherent cross-border regionalization are making inroads in the trading of renewable energy certificates (RECs). In the financing of climate resilient and carbon-free energy sources, RECs have had a 30-year-long tradition as tightly regulated but geographically open tender. Today powerful institutional drivers seek investments close to local markets. In this sense, the Guarantees of Origin (GoO) as defined in Article 15 of the European Directive 2009/28/EC in renewable energy certificates or other bi- or multilateral trading regimes have defined preferred arrangements among large and small purchasers and purveyors of clean energy credits.

Cultural, ethical, legal, and institutional factors are decisive drivers for international differences in supply and demand for sustainable investments across countries. Cross-border regions could play a pivotal role in stimulating demand for sustainable investments in the partner region across the border. Sustainable financial services can be freely offered across borders. This is especially the case for financial services within the European Union (McCormick. 2014). While this in itself does not offer resilience and may indeed contribute to the brittleness of the global financial system, it does imply the possibility and promise of a rise in regionally based but broadly accessible funding vehicles and even raises the virtue and utility of regional currency markets and nonmonetary exchange systems. As a result of cross-border benefit and effects, sustainable investments could develop more consistently all over the world, at various levels.

The movement toward sustainability is quite different in different political systems, and sustainable financial markets in local regional and cross-border regions could contribute an additional stimulus for all countries sharing a common resource base, such as water and renewable energy, and a common future in climatic paths and trajectories. Here community currencies indeed show a path into a shared and resilient future since they can link sustainability objectives, long-term future returns, and commitment to local regional and cross-border resilience (Ruddick 2022).

5 Discussion

Grounded in our description of some of the key dimensions relevant for creating resilient regions, we now provide a framework that allows the analysis of the emergence and enactment of regional affordances for resilience and sustainability in cross-border regions.

The model suggests that regional affordances emerge as relations between regional resources, institutional elements, and regional actors. *Regional resources* describe a region's stocks of assets (both material and nonmaterial) that actors can draw on to perform action, including natural (e.g., biospheric goods and services), economic (e.g., assets), social (e.g., networks), and technological (e.g., digital infrastructure) elements. The *actors*—representing key institutional orders such as in terms of organization, market, government, community, and family—identify action potentials that allow for decreasing failure probability, reducing consequences from failures, and allowing for short recovery times (Rose 2007). They do so within some *institutional context* that provides the regulative, normative, and cultural-cognitive elements that pattern action (Scott 2013). Regulative elements regularize and constrain behavior; normative elements represent the rules by which social behavior happens; and cultural-cognitive elements represent shared mental models constituting social reality (Scott 2013).

The model highlights (a) that multiple resources can be combined to create multiple regional affordances and resulting practices and (b) that the identification and enactment of affordances is contingent on broader, and often pluralistic, institutional contexts that regional actors draw on and are embedded in.

But why do organizational actors deliberately create and enact affordances to foster regional resilience? They do so as they perceive regional resources under consideration of their action goals, as they draw on some institutional context. Therefore, the specific values, goals, and norms that exist and actors draw on are important—as we indicated earlier. A shared vision needs to exist among change agents to accomplish regional resilience. This is a challenge considering how economic activity takes place in the pluralistic and overlapping institutional contexts we discussed—and as regions can cut through political systems. Such pluralism creates particular challenges for the implementation of resilient regions in situations when there is a goal conflict. For instance, actors representing the corporate order may draw on environmentalist as well as on market-based institutions, and these are likely to compete as they are associated with different goals (Dahlmann and Grosvold 2017). Regional affordances for civic involvement, engagement, and learning can help address this issue.

It is noteworthy that also the distinction between institutional elements and regional resources is analytical and that one could provide alternative conceptualizations. First, certain elements of the institutional context constitute regional resources in themselves (such as regional regulations and policies). Second, regional resources will act as carriers of institutional elements, such as when artifacts support certain practices consistent with some institutions, while they do not support others (Scott 2013). However, from an analytical standpoint, the following question is important: what affordances do regional actors identify for resilient practices as they interpret available resources under consideration of their institutional context? This question reflects the idea that affordances are not only relations between objects and actors but indeed between objects, actors, and institutional elements (Essén and Värlander 2019; Seidel and Berente 2013). At a general level, our model represents ideas of interrelated structures and agencies, where structures can be both material and social.

We view regional affordances as evolutionary—that is, they result from the intertwining of human agencies, regional resources, and the institutional context over time. This approach allows us to account for the flexible, dynamic processes that exist in urban and regional contexts and that provide the ground for collective reorganization and repositioning over time in the face of future internal and external disruptions. Figure 1 visualizes these ideas.

In this chapter, we have focused on those regional affordances that can help regional actors to provide appropriate responses to the various risks and challenges to regional resilience and thus help them react to both regional endogenous (e.g., infrastructural failure) and exogenous (e.g., originating from the global energy market) disturbances. Enacting these affordances can lead to different interrelated categories of practices—practices in the public sector of economic and social activity, practices in the for-profit sector of production and consumption, practices in the household sector of economic and social activity, practices in the not-for-profit sector of economic and social activity—and any combination thereof.

Table 1 provides an overview of key affordances we have described along with some examples we mentioned. These examples highlight the interplay of the elements of actor, institutions, and regional resources. For instance, learning and innovation affordances require (1) the technological as well as economic resources (e.g., in terms of digital infrastructures for exchange); (2) a suitable institutional context that provides the regulative, normative, and cultural-cognitive conditions for civic engagement (e.g., cultural-cognitive elements that frame collective action as desirable); and (3) the active participation of actors (which in turn requires some shared vision among actors).

Note how we are not aiming for exhaustiveness with this account. As the question of what constitutes a region is purely analytical, so is the question of what constitutes a regional affordance—and what regional affordances exist or perhaps should exist. What we did imply, however, is that these affordances must be

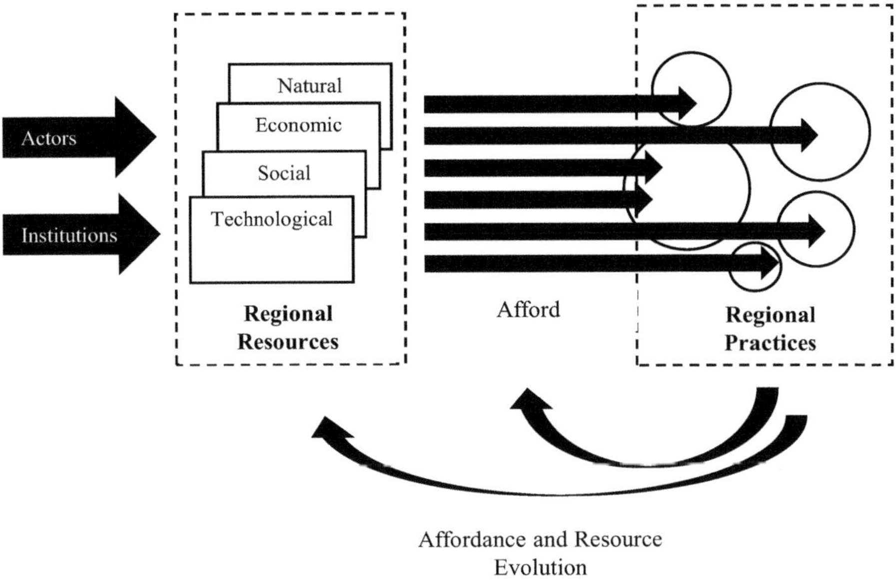

Fig. 1 Regional affordances

Table 1 Regional affordances

Affordance	Examples
Regional learning and innovation	Institutional, industrial, and civic involvement, engagement, and learning, achievable through collaborative processes to plan and implement change (Wolfe 2010)
Regional coordination	Local government incentives on energy efficiency and renewable energy
Regional measurement and control	Managing supply- and demand-side intermittency, since the transition toward the use of renewable energy requires key actions, for instance, in terms of managing deferrables (i.e., deferring the operation of devices to match supply and demand) or dynamic pricing (i.e., determining real-time prices for balancing supply and demand) (Watson et al. 2020) Measurement of regional carrying capacities
Regional energetic resilience	Accounting for both the self-sustaining supply and demand aspects within the regional renewable energy system
Regional economic resilience	Maintaining a diverse and well-networked ecosystem of information markets
Regional sustainable finance	Cross-border regions could play a pivotal role in stimulating demand for sustainable investments in the underdeveloped region across the border

identified and can be combined and that they can complement each other. This became visible, for instance, in our account of regional energetic resilience. Clearly, for regions to implement energetic resilience requires an informational basis for supply and demand and an appropriate institutional context that supports rights markets, as well as appropriate technological infrastructures. The model thus provides an analytical lens that allows us to ask various questions that, in turn, guide design processes and decisions.

First, the framework helps identify existing regional affordances and associated practices. One important question is:

What are the regional affordances for resilience that are currently enacted (in the public sector, in the private sector)?

Second, the framework helps identify potential areas of intervention. One important question is:

How can governments support the creation and emergence of regional affordances that provide the potential for the enactment of resilient regional practices?

Third, current natural and technological resources may be explored to identify further affordances that allow for practices that foster regional resilience. One may ask:

What are regional affordances that existing configurations of natural, economic, social, and technological could provide under consideration of the new goal of regional resilience?

How can these spaces be made visible to regional actors?

Creating resilient communities is a multidimensional challenge involving material and symbolic elements and based on the implementation and evolution of both physical and informational infrastructures.

6 Conclusion

In this chapter, we have described the concept of regional affordances to account for actionable spaces to secure and increase resilience within regional contexts. Regional affordances are based on natural, social, economic, and technological resources provided by a region to its communities, and they are enacted as actors perceive them to be consistent with their action goals within some institutional context. We have specifically focused our attention on sustainable development and resilience in a regional, cross-border context.

References

Akademie für Raumforschung und Landesplanung (1994) Perspektiven der Entwicklung ländlicher Räume in Deutschland. Hanover, Konzepte und Empfehlungen für die Landes-, Regional- und Kommunalplanung

Beniger J (2009) The control revolution: technological and economic origins of the information society. Harvard University Press, Cambridge, MA

Berkes F (1999) Sacred ecology: traditional ecological knowledge and resource management. Taylor and Francis, Ann Arbor, MI

Bernard HR (1992) Preserving language diversity. Hum Organ 51(1):82–89

Blum H, Legey LF (2012) The challenging economics of energy security: ensuring energy benefits in support to sustainable development. Energy Econ 34(6):1982–1989

Boesch M (1989) Engagierte Geographie. Zur Rekonstruktion der Raumwissenschaft als politikorientierte Geographie, vol 98. Franz Steiner Verlag, Stuttgart, Germany

Bridge G, Bouzarovski S, Bradshaw M, Eyre N (2013) Geographies of energy transition: space, place and the low-carbon economy. Energy Policy 53:331–340

Briguglio L, Cordina G, Farrugia N, Vella S (2009) Economic vulnerability and resilience: con cepts and measurements. Oxf Dev Stud 37(3):229–247

Bristow G, Healy A (2014) Regional resilience: an agency perspective. Reg Stud 48(5):923–935

Cecchetti SG, Schoenholtz KL (2011) Money, banking, and financial markets, 4th edn. McGraw-Hill Irwin, Boston

Christopherson S, Michie J, Tyler P (2010) Regional resilience: theoretical and empirical perspectives. Camb J Reg Econ Soc 3(1):3–10

Common M (1995) Sustainability and policy: limits to economics. Cambridge University Press, Cambridge, UK

Cooke P, Bristow G, Porter J (2011) Regional resilience literature review. Bordeaux, France

Crichton D, Nicol F, Roaf S (2009) Adapting buildings and cities for climate change. Routledge, New York

Dahlmann F, Grosvold J (2017) Environmental managers and institutional work: reconciling tensions of competing institutional logics. Bus Ethics Q 27(2):263–291

Daly HE (1999) Globalization versus internationalization - some implications. Ecol Econ 31(1):31–37

Droege P (2006) The renewable city: a comprehensive guide to an urban revolution. Wiley-Academy, Chichester, UK

Droege P (ed) (2014) Regenerative Region - Energie- und Klimaatlas Boensee-Alpenrhein. Oekom, Munich

Essén A, Värlander SW (2019) How technology afforded practices at the micro-level can generate change at the field level: theorizing the recursive mechanism actualized in Swedish rheumatology 2000-2014. MIS Q 43(4):1155–1176

Gibson JJ (1977) The theory of affordances. In: Shaw R, Bransford J (eds) Perceiving, acting and knowing: toward an ecological psychology. Lawrence Erlbaum Associates, Hillsdale, pp 67–82

Gibson JJ (1979) The theory of affordances. In: The ecological approach to visual perception. Lawrence Erlbaum Associates, Hillsdale, pp 127–143

Gosh DK, Ariff M (2014) Regional financial markets. Praeger Publishers, Westport

Hassink R (2010) Regional resilience: a promising concept to explain differences in regional economic adaptability? Camb J Reg Econ Soc 3(1):45–58

Holling CS (1973) Resilience and stability of ecological systems. Annu Rev Ecol Syst 4(1):1–23

Hudson R (2010) Resilient regions in an uncertain world: wishful thinking or a practical reality? Camb J Reg Econ Soc 3(1):11–25

IPCC - Intergovernmental Panel on Climate Change (2022) Climate change 2022 - impacts, adaptation and vulnerability. Working Group II contribution to the Sixth Assessment of the Intergovernmental Panel on Climate Change. Summary for Policymakers. Pages 35 and 36. IPCC, Geneva. https://www.ipcc.ch/report/ar6/wg2/. Retrieved 28 February 2022

Kiernan MJ (2009) Investing in a sustainable world. AMACOM, New York
Maffi L (1998) Language: a resource for nature. Nat Resour 34(4):12–21
Magis K (2010) Community resilience: an indicator of social sustainability. Soc Nat Resour 23(5):401–416
Martin R, Sunley P (2015) On the notion of regional economic resilience: conceptualization and explanation. J Econ Geogr 15(1):1–42
McCormick. (2014) Understanding the European Union. Palgrave Macmillan, Hampshire
Mishkin FS, Eakins SG (2016) Financial markets and institutions, 8th edn. Pearson, Boston, MA
Oxford English Dictionary (2010a) "resilience, n." Oxford University Press, Oxford, UK
Oxford English Dictionary (2010b) "risk, n." Oxford University Press, Oxford, UK
Pendall R, Foster KA, Cowell M (2010) Resilience and regions: building understanding of the metaphor. Camb J Reg Econ Soc 3(1):71–84
Perrings C (1998) Resilience in the dynamics of economy-environment systems. Environ Resour Econ 11(3):503–520
Perrings C (2001) 13. Resilience and sustainability. In: Folmer H, Gabel HL, Gerking S, Rose A (eds) Frontiers of environmental economics. Edward Elgar, Cheltenham, UK, pp 319–342
Prior T, Hagmann J (2014) Measuring resilience: methodological and political challenges of a trend security concept. J Risk Res 17(3):281–298
Rees W, Wackernagel M (1994) Ecological footprints and appropriated carrying capacity: measuring the natural capital requirements of the human economy. In: Jansson A-M, Hammer M, Folke C, Costanza R (eds) Investing in natural capital: the ecological economics approach to sustainability. Island Press, Washington, DC
Rees W, Wackernagel M (1996) Urban ecological footprints: why cities cannot be sustainable – and why they are a key to sustainability. Environ Impact Assess Rev 16:223–248
Reggiani A, De Graaff T, Nijkamp P (2002) Resilience: an evolutionary approach to spatial economic systems. Netw Spat Econ 2(2):211–229
Rose A (2007) Economic resilience to natural and man-made disasters: multidisciplinary origins and contextual dimensions. Environ Hazards 7(4):383–398
Ruddick WO (2022) Community inclusion currencies. In: Droege P (ed) Intelligent environments: advanced systems for a healthy planet. Elsevier, New York
Scott WR (2013) Institutions and organizations: ideas, interests, and identities. Sage, New York
Seidel S, Berente N (2013) Toward" third wave" information systems research: linking sociomaterial practice with broader institutional logics. In: Proceedings of the 34th International Conference on Information Systems, Milan, Italy
Stern N (2006) The economics of climate change: the stern review. Cambridge University Press, Cambridge, MA
Terkenli TS (1995) Home as a region. Geographical Review 1995:324–334
UNFCC (2016) The Paris climate agreement. https://unfccc.int/files/meetings/paris_nov_2015/application/pdf/paris_agreement_english_.pdf
United Nations (2016) Sustainable development goals. https://www.un.org/sustainabledevelopment/sustainable-development-goals/
Walker B, Gunderson L, Kinzig A, Folke C, Carpenter S, Schultz L (2006) A handful of heuristics and some propositions for understanding resilience in social-ecological systems. Ecol Soc 11(1)
Watson RT, Boudreau MC, Chen AJ (2010) Information systems and environmentally sustainable development: energy informatics and new directions for the IS community. MIS Q 2010:23–38
Watson RT, Ketter W, Recker J, Seidel S (2020) Transitioning to intermittent energy: the critical digital transformation of the decade. Available at SSRN 3737738
Wiechmann T (2000) Die Region ist tot—es lebe die Region! Raumforschung und Raumordnung 58(2):173–184
Wolfe DA (2010) The strategic management of core cities: path dependence and economic adjustment in resilient regions. Camb J Reg Econ Soc 3(1):139–152
Zolli A, Healy A (2012) Resilience: why things bounce back. Headline Publishing Group, London

Site Selection According to Life Cycles in Agglomeration Areas: A Dynamic and Interdisciplinary Location Analysis of the Four-Country-Region Lake Constance-Alpine Rhine Valley

Stefan Güldenberg, Laura Hecker, Adrian Klammer, Francesco A. Schurr, Peter Staub, and Stefan Wilhelm

Abstract This chapter summarizes the main findings of one of the first empirical studies that outline the differences and similarities arising in polycentric border-crossing agglomerations in a knowledge-based economy. In our study, we examine the multi-country border-crossing polycentric agglomeration in the Lake Constance-Alpine Rhine Valley region, comprised of Liechtenstein and parts of Austria, Germany, and Switzerland. We specifically try to identify factors influencing the residential choice within a polycentric border-crossing agglomeration in a knowledge-based economy. Although the results and outcomes are limited to the case study region, the implications could be tested in other polycentric border-

An earlier version of this chapter was published as Güldenberg et al. (2017).

S. Güldenberg (✉)
EHL Hospitality Business School, HES-SO, Lausanne, Switzerland
e-mail: stefan.guldenberg@ehl.ch

L. Hecker
Delivery Hero SE, Berlin, Germany
e-mail: laura.hecker@deliveryhero.com

A. Klammer
Nova Consulting, Vaduz, Liechtenstein
e-mail: adrian.klammer@nova-consulting.li

F. A. Schurr
University of Innsbruck, Innsbruck, Austria
e-mail: francesco.schurr@uibk.ac.at

P. Staub
Bern University of Applied Sciences, Bern, Switzerland
e-mail: peter.staub@bfh.ch

S. Wilhelm
University of Liechtenstein, Vaduz, Liechtenstein
e-mail: stefan.wilhelm@uni.li

P. Droege et al. (eds.), *Cross-Border Life and Work*, Contributions to Management Science, https://doi.org/10.1007/978-3-031-34362-9_2

crossing agglomerations characterized by knowledge-based economies across the globe. Our results reveal that the most important factors for residential choice are proximity to family and friends, safety, career opportunities, and a high standard of living.

1 Introduction

The future of life and work is currently characterized by many contradictions and challenges. The COVID-19 pandemic at the beginning of the 2020s accelerated several trends like increased digitalization, automation, e-commerce, and remote work (Güldenberg et al. 2021). Most importantly, it triggered policy and sentiment shifts within Europe and elsewhere that led many societies to question their life and work cultures. It also demonstrated the importance of open borders for our global economy and the very different regional approaches within Europe to deal with the pandemic successfully.

What does this mean for a microstate such as Liechtenstein, and how should it position itself within Europe, a continent that is characterized by contradictions and in which people and enterprises become more and more mobile? For what sorts of people does Liechtenstein wish to be attractive in the future, and what kinds of collaboration does it need with its surrounding region of the Lake Constance-Alpine Rhine Valley? How can negative scenarios such as emigration, over-indebtedness, and "over-aging" be prevented while simultaneously assuring a sustainable development of Liechtenstein's economy and society?

By choosing a dynamic and interdisciplinary approach, we want to contribute to the literature of border-crossing agglomerations. To this date, it has not yet been sufficiently researched which factors constitute a successful collaboration, sustainable development, and long-lasting prosperity of border-crossing agglomerations in a knowledge-based economy. Therefore, this paper tries to narrow down this research gap by addressing the following two main research questions:

Q1: What are success factors for competitiveness of a border-crossing agglomeration across all stages of life?

Q2: Which criteria—depending on respective phases of life (education, career entry, career advancement, start of a family, end of career, and retirement)—play decisive roles when choosing locations?

The topic will be approached and examined from different academic perspectives, including architecture and planning, business administration, law (statutory law and case law), economics, and other social sciences. By applying a threefold approach, this paper firstly explains its theoretical framework. Thereafter, the methodology underlying the quantitative study is introduced. Thirdly, key results are outlined and discussed.

2 Theoretical Framework

The following section provides the theoretical background of the paper by reviewing the existing literature on the topic. After briefly introducing the terms and concepts of polycentric and monocentric areas, regional development, knowledge work, and the creative class, a primary focus is placed on the description of different location and site selection factors.

2.1 *Monocentric and Polycentric Areas*

In general terms, cities and areas of living are differentiated into two different models: monocentric and polycentric areas. However, consistent criteria for classifying an area as either monocentric or polycentric are missing in the academic literature (Kloosterman and Musterd 2001). An area is considered to be monocentric, when cities are formed around one center called central business district (CBD) which employs a city's whole labor force (Ogawa and Fujita 1980; Oueslati et al. 2015). Consequently, in monocentric cities, businesses prefer to locate within the city's CBD. However, some researchers argue that the monocentric approach does not account for the requirements of modern cities and societies (Kloosterman and Musterd 2001; Ogawa and Fujita 1980; Wheaton 2004). Contrastingly, Arribas-Bel and Sanz-Gracia (2014) conclude that monocentric city models are predominantly present within North American metropolitan regions. A further study conducted by the German Federal Institute for Research on Building, Urban Affairs and Spatial Development (BBSR) (BBSR 2011) states that out of 184 locations with metropolitan functions, 94 were considered as being monocentric.

Furthermore, polycentric urban areas are defined as large areas with several subcenters of employment distributed in different parts of the area or city forming various concentrations of inhabitants and businesses. Kloosterman and Musterd (2001) distinguish between two different types of polycentricity. One model refers to the intra-urban pattern of economic and population clusters within one large city, whereas the second describes interurban patterns of different cities networking in collaboration. Additionally, Kloosterman and Lambregts (2001) highlight the following three characteristics of polycentric urban regions: (i) they consist of a number of historically distinct cities which are located within commuting distances; (ii) they lack a clear leading city being dominant in political, economic, cultural, and other aspects, but they rather tend to consist of a few larger cities that do not greatly differ in terms of size and overall economic importance and many smaller cities; and (iii) the member cities are not only spatially distinct but also constitute independent political entities. Consequently, many researchers regard the concept of polycentric urban regions as more modern and better suited for urban modeling (Meijers et al. 2012). Although polycentric urban areas lack a single CBD, clusters of highly specialized industries within an area are formed in order to generate comparative advantage and to attract skilled employees. Furthermore, regional companies' strategies tend to assimilate over time, and consequently, highly specialized clusters are formed in order to gain competitive advantages (Kloosterman and Lambregts 2001).

Concluding, often quoted practical examples for European border-crossing monocentric agglomerations in Europe are Øresund, Strasbourg, and Triest, whereas Singapore represents the best-known international example. Furthermore, border-crossing polycentric agglomerations can be found in the Euregio Mass-Rhein, RegioTriRhena, and Saar-Lor-Lux, as well as in the Lake Constance-Alpine Rhine Valley.

2.2 Regional Development and Attractiveness in a Knowledge Economy

Moreover, both monocentric and polycentric agglomerations are forced to enhance and expand their regional development to stay attractive and competitive. The Organisation for Economic Co-operation and Development (OECD) defines regional development as the "general effort to reduce regional disparities by supporting (employment and wealth-generating) economic activities in regions" (OECD 2016). Furthermore, the OECD states that regional development is currently undergoing structural change, as it had been observed that past approaches failed to diminish differences among regions. Additionally, the OECD outlines that previous strategies were not capable of reducing regional disparities and supporting single regions to make progress although they were supported with public funding. Therefore, they introduced a new comprehensive approach for regional development, which targets to use public resources more efficiently by focusing on an increase of competitiveness of all regions instead of redistributing financial resources and subsidies. Moreover, this new approach intends, inter alia, to introduce a strategy for development which includes a broad scope of direct as well as indirect factors concerning the performance of local companies and an enhanced focus on regional specific assets rather than top-down transfers or investments (OECD 2016).

2.3 Knowledge Work and the Creative Class as the Future

Knowledge is considered a crucial factor for regional development, as knowledge is an essential source of creating value within firms. Knowledge work, defined as the contribution of knowledge to the value added, is often considered to be more beneficial than manual work. Moreover, as society transforms from an industry-oriented to a knowledge-oriented one, an increasing amount of workforce is attributed to knowledge-intensive and creative professions such as consulting, teaching, management, journalism, or social careers (North and Güldenberg 2011). According to

Florida (2002), these observed societal changes affect the way how people work, resulting in the rise of a new social stratum referred to as the creative class, whose values comprise creativity, performance orientation, individuality, and uniqueness. Florida's approach is frequently summarized as a picture of young professionals seeking an adequate work-life balance and settling in a creative center or a culturally diverse urban area. Moreover, the author highlights that companies are following young professionals to certain cities. This assumption is contrary to existing theories, which assume that employees are the ones who move. Florida's assumption is predominantly based on the idea that postindustrial cities are forced to attract creative and qualified young professionals in the international war for talent in order to sustain and enhance their competitiveness. Additionally, the availability of a highly qualified workforce in a certain area might encourage companies to settle in these regions, which adds further value to the area creating upward momentum and enhancing regional competition for brain gain (North and Güldenberg 2011).

2.4 Site Selection and Location Factors

Taking the global war for talent into account, the question arises which factors are essential for an appropriate regional development and the attraction of knowledge workers to an area. Since knowledge workers are important drivers of economic growth, an increased interest in the concept of knowledge cities and knowledge-based urban development emerged during the last two decades. Florida (2002) combines creative class clusters with indices of regional attractiveness. He highlights that knowledge workers' requirements for an attractive area differ from traditional ones. Moreover, Carrillo et al. (2007) state that for knowledge workers, especially educational offers, leisure and cultural activities as well as an adequate wage level are important site selection factors. Additionally, the authors also mention classical location factors such as the availability of public transport systems and infrastructure or the affordability of housing. Furthermore, in their work, Frenkel et al. (2013) examine the actual residential location preferences of knowledge workers. Their study intends to bridge the gap between conceptual approaches of knowledge workers' residential choice and classical location choice theory. They conclude that the socioeconomic level, which is considered as a proxy for well-off knowledge communities, and housing affordability are the most influential location factors for knowledge workers, followed by commute travel time as well as travel time to the central business district (CBD). Moreover, characteristics such as population density or cultural and educational land use are considered as decisive location factors. Nevertheless, Frenkel et al.'s study provides evidence that, concerning individual characteristics, activity patterns have a significant impact. For example, a culture-oriented pattern facilitates residence in an inner-city location, whereas a home-oriented activity pattern creates preference for living in the suburbs or outer rings of a metropolitan area. These findings coincide with previous studies emphasizing the importance of classical location factors for knowledge worker's residential location decisions. However, their study highlights that, contrary to Florida's work, housing affordability is one of the most decisive location factors, whose importance has significantly increased since the financial crisis. Moreover, they find that knowledge worker's location decisions are substantially influenced by their culture-oriented leisure activity patterns, conforming Florida's (2002) and Yigitcanlar et al.'s (2007) approach. Finally, Frenkel et al. (2013) conclude that knowledge workers cannot be considered as a homogeneous group.

In general, territorial attractiveness is defined as the region's ability to attract and maintain various economic as well as mobile factors of production activities, which comprise, inter alia, businesses, professional events, entrepreneurs, or capital. Furthermore, local attractiveness is considered as a reflection of the region's performance in a certain period of time. Additionally, the concept of regional attractiveness is increasingly integrated into local elected positions and their development services explaining and justifying the choice of investments and new activities for developing a city or a conurbation. Therefore, policies aim to attract both, exogenous and endogenous, investments in an area increasing the level of economic activity (Capello et al. 2011). In this context, the study conducted by Brown et al. (2008) should be emphasized as an exemplary empirical work focusing on key attractiveness factors of a monocentric agglomeration. Within their study, several key factors including the availability of higher education facilities, transportation services, location, social diversity of people, culture, leisure, and entertainment offers were analyzed. Additionally, the Birmingham study illustrates how an urban agglomeration can develop from a manufacturing-oriented into a service-oriented region. Hence, the Birmingham case is regarded as a best practice example for an urban development policy which emphasizes on the one hand the importance of knowledge workers and on the other hand increases the region's attractiveness for inhabitants and their satisfaction with existing working and living environments.

Furthermore, local attractiveness is crucial for companies to settle in a region. Business location factors are utmost important in companies' site selection as this decision strongly impacts a firm's success. Site selection is omnipresent in the relocation and decision process as it has a long-term impact on the companies' ventures. Jirásková and Žižka (2011) emphasize that location decisions influence a company's success and are thus, in combination with spatial orientation, essential for ensuring long-term profits. According to them, various business location factors, which are exposed to constant change, as new factors might appear while existing ones may disappear, exist. The academic literature differentiates between classical (hard) and modern (soft) factors which can be denoted as economic and quality of life factors or as measurable and nonmeasurable factors (Laulajainen and Stafford 2013; Płaziak and Szymańska 2014).

Moreover, in the literature, it is emphasized that many border-crossing polycentric agglomerations face problems arising from legal frameworks for cross-border activities, as legal structures are not centrally provided for an area but are rather determined on a local basis by national or regional governments. For businesses and employees, this issue becomes particularly severe if not all jurisdictions of an agglomeration area belong to the same area of supranational law such as the

European Union. Additionally, legal issues could arise whenever a microstate such as Liechtenstein is squeezed in between larger countries and thus strives on preserving its sovereignty under the pressure of national and regional legal harmonization.

3 Methodology and Case

3.1 The Four-Country-Region Lake Constance-Alpine Rhine Valley

According to Scharting et al. (2008), the four-country-region Lake Constance-Alpine Rhine Valley includes Switzerland, the Principality of Liechtenstein, Germany, and Austria. The Lake Constance-Alpine Rhine Valley extends over a length of about 90 km from the confluence of the Anterior Rhine and Posterior Rhine to the mouth of the Rhine in Lake Constance. For the purpose of better understandability and easiness of reading, we refer to the described region simply as the Alpine Rhine Valley (ARV).

The ARV is regarded as a flourishing economic region. Especially the process of industrialization in the nineteenth century and the tertiarization in the twentieth century has strongly characterized this region, making the region an attractive area of settlement for both multinational enterprises (MNEs) and small and medium sized enterprises (SMEs) (Scharting et al. 2008). As a consequence of the agglomeration of these highly modern industrial companies, the ARV gained popularity as a region with a high degree of differentiation and specialization. In addition to these industrial characteristics, Liechtenstein is a major center that creates a remarkable number of new jobs (Schlegel 2009).

Besides economic conditions, leisure time and culture are very important factors for determining the attractiveness of cities or regions. Obkircher (2011) suggests that the inhabitants of the ARV value the wide range of cultural activities as well as leisure time opportunities. The cooperation Kulturachse: Bregenz-St. Gallen-Vaduz-Chur, a partnership between Kunsthaus Bregenz, Kunstmuseum St. Gallen, Kunstmuseum Liechtenstein, and Bündner Kunstmuseum Chur, illustrates the importance of (cross-border) culture in the region.

For an attractive region, it is no longer only important to have a lot of companies that generate profit but also to attract potential employees with a good infrastructure and accessibility. Sieverts (2012) describes the ARV as an interurban (polycentric) structure without a dominant center. Obkircher (2011) adds that good infrastructure and accessibility is also supported by the ability to cross borders without any problems, as currently seen in the ARV. Although located in a highly natural area with mountains, rivers, and lakes, the region is well connected to major cities, such as Zurich, Munich, Stuttgart, Innsbruck, and Milan, all of which are within 3 hours' driving time.

Obkircher (2011) discusses how inhabitants of the ARV perceive their environment and how national borders influence the transborder cooperation and their life. The main differences between the nations Austria, Liechtenstein, Switzerland, and Germany are the different price levels and attitudes for quality (Obkircher 2011). According to Simon and Wyssen (2011), the main advantages of the region are the attractive tax system, recreational value, as well as a location that combines the borders of Switzerland, Germany, Liechtenstein, and Austria. The main disadvantages of the ARV are the limited labor market for skilled workers and academics, the restricted versatility of branches, and the huge differences in the wage levels between the four regions.

Focusing on the creative industry in the ARV, Staub et al. (2014) describe the region as a significant growth market and driver for innovations. Today, efficiency, productivity, and effectiveness are a necessity, but not a sufficient condition for growth. Especially joined-up thinking and being open minded have gained huge importance, which is why the creative industry has great potential for the future. For people working in the creative industry, the compatibility of work and private life has to be ensured (Staub et al. 2014). Moreover, values such as work-life balance, training opportunities, and flexibility have to be taken into consideration as well (Hunnius 2015).

3.2 *Case Study Methodology*

3.2.1 Research Method

We examined the relevant research questions by sending out an online questionnaire to randomly selected participants within the ARV. We sent out e-mails including a link to the questionnaire that was created with the online tool umfrageonline.com. In doing so, we were allowed to target participants from various age groups, from different functional and educational backgrounds (employed or unemployed), living and working within the countries that comprise the ARV.

Due to the interdisciplinary nature of the research objectives, our questionnaire consists of various categories. The first part aims at the respondents' demographic characteristics. This demographic part allows us to categorize the respondents according to country of residence, gender, age group, educational background, etc. The second part of the questionnaire is directed toward answering the actual research questions. Survey items of this part target to examine the current (perceived) status quo as well as the desired attractiveness of the ARV region. Moreover, the questionnaire surveys several important business location factors (including satisfaction with the respective taxation and legal systems of the specific countries). In addition, respondents are asked to provide answers to their current and desired work-life balance.

We then analyze the given answers by means of descriptive statistics and frequency analysis in order to juxtapose the status quo and the desired conditions of business locations factors, attractiveness of the region, and work-life balance of the respondents. Subsequently, we use these results as a foundation for the discussion section.

3.2.2 Sample

Prior to the publication of the final questionnaire, pretests were conducted in order to detect potential mistakes and ensure comprehensibility of the survey. After adjusting the questionnaire, the collection of data began. The survey was sent to participants via e-mail and was available online from April through May 2016. Five hundred eighty-one respondents participated in the online survey. However, only 432 individuals fully completed the questionnaire. Hence, approximately 25% of the questionnaire needed to be omitted due to insufficient data. These 432 fully answered questionnaires were used for analysis.

Out of these, 42.9% indicate that they live in Austria, 29.1% in Liechtenstein, 16.1% in Switzerland, and 11.9% in Germany. In relation to the population distribution (Statistikplattform Bodensee 2021), respondents from Germany and Switzerland seem to be underrepresented in the sample. Most respondents (78.6%) suggest that they would describe the region in which they live as rural. This result is not surprising since the ARV is classified as a peripheral center (Kuehn 2016). The ratio of male and female respondents is almost balanced with 53.4% to 46.6%. In terms of age distribution, 30.7% of respondents lie in the age group of below 25-year-olds, 22.1% from 25 to 35 years, 15.4% from 36 to 45 years, 23.2% from 46 to 55 years, 7.6% from 56 to 65 years, and 1% 65 years and above. This suggests that 52.8% of respondents can be categorized as Generation Y, 38.6% as Generation X, and 8.6% as baby boomers. This corresponds with the age structure of the population in the ARV region (Statistikplattform Bodensee 2021).

4 Results

4.1 Principality of Liechtenstein

Respondents from Liechtenstein provided 112 fully answered and valid questionnaires. Both, the age group of under 25-year-olds and the 25- to 35-year-olds, each made up approximately 21% of the responses. The age group 36 to 45 years accounts for about 13% of the answers. The 46- to 55-year-old participants represent the largest group with about 30%. The age group of 56 to 65 years makes up about 14%, whereas only 1% of the answers come from over 65-year-olds. Out of these fully answered questionnaires, about 57% are male and 43% are female respondents.

The main reasons why people live in Liechtenstein are quite obvious. Most of the respondents state that they were born and raised in Liechtenstein and have all their family and friends in the region. Another essential factor for people living in Liechtenstein is the high security standard of the ARV region. A significant number of respondents also acknowledge the proximity to nature and mountains as well as the high density of ski slopes as an important factor of why they live in the ARV. Since the region in and around Liechtenstein is famous for its numerous possibilities of sportive activities, it is not surprising that the participants are highly satisfied with these kinds of offerings. Also, cultural and leisure time activities, gastronomy, social activities, and infrastructure receive high praise. Moreover, people are highly content with the landscape and the family friendliness in the region. People are mainly satisfied in terms of career opportunities and the overall economic situation in Liechtenstein as well as the reputation of the region. The overall quality of life and the level of security are highly ranked and can therefore be seen as the most important aspects for the inhabitants.

On the contrary, Liechtenstein's inhabitants are not satisfied with the availability of building land as well as with the affordability of living space, such as flats or houses. This might be due to the extremely high living costs in the region. Although Liechtenstein has one of the highest wage levels in Europe, it is also one of the most expensive countries in Europe to live in. General living costs, electricity, transportation, mandatory health insurance, and other fixed costs consume a lot of a person's average income.

In general, the results indicate that the respondents are satisfied with current laws, such as civil law, family law, or taxation, in Liechtenstein.

4.2 Austria

Participants from Austria provided 186 fully answered questionnaires. The under 25-year-olds were the most represented age group with approximately 38%. Respondents of the age group 25 to 35 years and 36 to 45 years made up 15% and 14%, respectively. With 27%, the 46- to 55-year-olds were the second largest group of participants. Respondents older than 56 years only account for 2% of the study. Male and female respondents are almost equally distributed.

People living in the Austrian part of the ARV are highly satisfied with the nature and landscape offered by the region. The mountains, rivers, lakes, and forests provide a great variety of terrain. Furthermore, the general living quality, security, and the possibility of sports and activities are valued. With regard to job and career opportunities, Austrian participants are very happy with their working environment, the success found in their jobs, and the possibility for pursuing further education. Quality of living, security, healthcare, and nature are significant factors when choosing a place to live. Austrian respondents regard the possibilities for taking own initiative in the workplace, working environment, wage, job security, and work-life balance as important factors when choosing a place of work. Career opportunities, wages, and the possibility to change jobs are rated as neutral. Respondents are less satisfied with the scarcity of places to build on real estate. Moreover, the affordability of living space is rated as unsatisfactory. The possibilities for social activities, abundance in building land, and the reputation of the region are the least important factors when choosing a place to live.

Austrian participants find that the attractiveness of the ARV can be enhanced by further improving the existing infrastructure and the creation of new jobs. They suggest that the region should be made more attractive to talents and new possible employees. Improving the possibilities for leisure time and cultural activities, healthcare, and political cooperation are perceived as the least important factors for enhancing the attractiveness of the ARV.

Although the majority of the respondents are satisfied or very satisfied with the (overall) legal framework, it stands out that about 40% of the participants answered that they are not satisfied with the laws on taxation in Austria.

4.3 Switzerland

The respondents from Switzerland provided 88 fully answered and valid questionnaires. A little bit more than half of the participants from Switzerland were under 25 years old. The second largest group with approximately 25% represented the age group 25- to 35-year-olds. The remaining quarter of respondents was comprised of 36-year-olds and above. The share of male and female participants was almost equal.

Participants from Switzerland highly ranked the level of security and living standard in the ARV. On the other side, they were less satisfied with the possibilities for social activities in the region. When asked to rank the most significant factors about their workplace and career, the respondents' priorities were clearly focused on possibilities for career development, communication and networking at work, salary, and a good working environment.

According to the respondents, Switzerland is appreciated for its beautiful lakes, biking trails, and hiking routes in the mountains. Aspects such as landscape, nature, and safety are very important for more than 80% of the respondents. The less important aspects for the participants were dining, shopping, infrastructure, and accessibility to and within the region. In general, respondents from Switzerland highly appreciate their quality of life as well as the level of safety in the region.

Most of Swiss participants are highly satisfied with the legislative situation. Although many of the respondents from Switzerland were satisfied with the overall laws, the satisfaction with tax laws revealed the lowest rate of satisfaction in comparison with other parts of law. Still, taxation in Switzerland remains one of the lowest in Europe, providing people with higher disposable income.

4.4 Germany

Forty-six participants fully answered the questionnaire. The age group below 25-year-olds accounted for more than a third of the respondents. The 25- to 35-year-olds made up around 27% of the participants from Germany. About 20% of the respondents were in the age group of 36 to 45 years. The 46- to 55-year-olds represented approximately 13% of the answered questionnaires. Around 4% of the answers came from the age group of 56- to 65-year-olds, whereas none of the respondents were older than 65 years. The gender distribution showed that about 70% of the participants were male and only 30% were female.

The two most important factors in terms of satisfaction with regard to the region the respondents live in were nature and landscape as well as the general quality of living. The German participants were least satisfied with the availability of building land and the affordability of housing. Regarding job satisfaction, respondents were most content with their job security and the feeling of succeeding in their jobs. On the other hand, German respondents were least satisfied with the salary as well as work-life balance. The results showed that the surveyed population was rather satisfied with their current life and job situation. Even the worst ratings were still in the average "neutral" category. While the satisfaction about the general legal framework as well as the family and civil law tended to be positive, the participants were clearly less satisfied with the taxation laws.

4.5 Comparison of the Four Regions

When considering the working situation in the ARV, a few differences between the countries Switzerland, Lichtenstein, Austria, and Germany became evident. Even though most people work in the same country they live in, there are a few cross-border commuters. Especially in Austria and in Switzerland, 29.4% and 36.1%, respectively, of people commute daily to Liechtenstein for work.

When considering how satisfied people are about different factors concerning their career, similarities between the countries of Liechtenstein/Switzerland and Austria/Germany can be perceived. Respondents from Liechtenstein and Switzerland were rather unsatisfied with the possibility to change their job and the opportunity for advancement in their career, even though they were satisfied with their working environment. In Austria and Germany, on the other hand, participants were rather unsatisfied with their current work-life balance and their level of salary. Austrian respondents were pleased with the working environment, whereas German participants were satisfied with the job security. The feeling of succeeding in their job was seen as a key satisfaction factor in both countries.

The four most important reasons why people live in the ARV only differ marginally from country to country. The four most important reasons why people from Liechtenstein live in the region were family and friends live here, standard of safety, born in the ARV, and good career perspectives. In Switzerland, the respondents provide similar answers as their most important factors are: family and friends live here, born in the ARV, standard of safety, availability of housing, and quality of living. Interestingly, Austrian respondents living in the ARV almost gave the exact same answers as participants from the previously described countries. The four most important factors were family and friends live here, born in the ARV, standard of safety, and good career perspectives. The answers from the German participants show great similarities to the other countries as their most important factors of why they live in the ARV were family and friends live here, good career perspectives, born in the ARV, and their job or their partner's job.

In all four countries, the answer that family and friends also live in the ARV was the primary reason for living in the ARV. Moreover, being born in the ARV ranks in the top 3 answers in all four countries. Furthermore, respondents from Liechtenstein, Germany, and Austria regard the standard of safety as a significant reason for living in the ARV. Participants from every country (except Switzerland) highly rank the good perspectives in terms of their career. We find almost no major differences between the countries regarding the four most important reasons why people live in the ARV.

When it comes to satisfaction with certain aspects in the Alpine Rhine Valley, there were many similarities but also a few differences among the four different country regions. People from Liechtenstein are currently most satisfied with the existing nature and scenery, safety, and general living standard. These three criteria were also important for the selection of the optimal place to live. Current and desired situations of people living in Liechtenstein are very similar. On the contrary, respondents from Liechtenstein were rather unsatisfied with the living costs, the availability of building land, and existing leisure time activities. Hence, they wish for an optimization of these areas of dissatisfaction.

Austrian respondents were very satisfied with nature and scenery, the general quality of life, and the availability and/or quality of existing sports activities. Similarly, the optimal place to live is closely the same as seen in the current situation. However, participants from Austria are not satisfied with the living costs, availability of building land, and the availability of social activities. Although social activities do not necessarily need to be improved, Austrian respondents call for a decrease of living costs as well as an increase in the availability of building land.

The situation in Switzerland is similar. Swiss respondents are very satisfied with nature and scenery, standard of safety, and general quality of living. These factors were also mentioned in their idea of the optimal place to live in. On the downside, Swiss participants were rather unhappy with current availability of social activities, availability of building land, as well as the possibilities for cultural activities. As a consequence, respondents from Switzerland called for an improvement to social and cultural activities.

The current situation in Germany appears to be very similar to the one in Austria. Respondents from Germany stated that they were very satisfied with nature and scenery, the overall quality of living, as well as the availability and/or quality of sports activities. The most important factors for the optimal place to live in go hand in hand with the current aspects. In contrast, German respondents seemed to be unhappy with the living costs, availability of building land, as well as availability and/or quality of social activities. Similar to Austria, the German participants desire a decrease in living costs and more availability of building land, whereas the availability and/or quality of social activities does not necessarily need to be improved.

When comparing and contrasting these four countries, we perceived no major differences when it came to the general satisfaction with specific aspects of a place to live. Mostly, respondents from all four countries were satisfied with nature and scenery, the overall quality of living, and the availability of sports activities. Individuals from all four countries mentioned the same most important reasons regarding the optimal place to live. Generally, the respondents were rather unhappy with the living costs, the current availability of building land, and the availability and/or quality of social activities. Table 1 illustrates the average current satisfaction rates (Likert scale from 1 = very dissatisfied to 5 = very satisfied) of participants of the respective countries and total respondents compared to the optimal (desired) situation.

We asked the participants to rate the legal conditions in both their country of residence and country of workplace. When questioned about the satisfaction of the general legal framework in their country of residence, respondents from Switzerland (3.81) and Liechtenstein (3.77) seemed to be most satisfied. In terms of taxation law, residents of Liechtenstein seemed to be the most content (3.82), while residents of Germany are clearly unsatisfied (2.62). Family law conditions in the various countries do not reveal any significant differences. Similar results can also be seen in terms of civil law. However, with a range from 3.67 (Liechtenstein) to 3.27 (Germany), the differences are more significant than in terms of family law. Table 2 shows the average values of satisfaction of the general legislation, taxation law, family law, and civil law in the respective countries of residence of the respondents.

Due to the high mobility of the inhabitants of the ARV, we also evaluate the legal frameworks in the respondents' country of workplace. Participants working in Switzerland (3.85) are most satisfied with the general legislation in the country of workplace, followed by Liechtenstein (3.74). Respondents working in Germany gave the lowest value (2.92) in terms of taxation law. Regarding labor and business law, Austria, Germany, and Switzerland showed similar results. Whereas individuals working in Liechtenstein seemed to be most satisfied with all types of legislation and law (no value is less than 3.72), the Germans are most dissatisfied (with a range from 2.92 to 3.40). Table 3 shows the average values of satisfaction of the general legislation, labor law, taxation law, and business law according to the countries of the participants' workplaces.

Table 1 Satisfaction of the ARV region. Current situation compared to the optimal/desired situation

	FL		CH		AT		DE		Total	
<	Current situation	Desired situation	Current situation	Desired situation	Current situation	Desired situation	Current situation	Desired situation	Current situation	Desired situation
Sports activities	4.45	3.95	4.11	4.00	**4.42**	3.99	**4.10**	4.09	**4.34**	3.99
Cultural activities	3.85	*3.64*	*3.12*	*3.29*	3.61	*3.55*	3.50	*3.22*	3.58	*3.49*
Leisure time activities	*3.44*	3.80	3.20	3.98	3.64	3.96	3.74	4.23	*3.52*	3.95
Gastronomy and shopping	3.63	4.08	3.81	4.16	3.82	4.05	3.88	4.11	3.77	4.09
Social activities	3.59	*3.48*	*3.10*	*3.43*	*3.50*	*3.39*	3.49	*3.45*	3.46	*3.43*
Infrastructure	3.96	4.10	3.43	4.00	3.90	4.25	3.74	4.11	3.82	4.15
Nature and scenery	**4.78**	**4.57**	**4.60**	**4.32**	**4.66**	**4.62**	**4.31**	4.34	**4.64**	**4.52**
Family-friendly environment	4.17	4.13	4.22	4.08	4.15	4.34	3.88	3.93	4.13	4.19
Health system	4.24	4.52	3.93	4.30	4.16	4.57	*3.62*	4.11	4.08	4.46
Possibility to live in a single-family home	3.80	3.80	3.75	3.72	3.75	3.94	*3.43*	4.12	3.73	3.89
Availability of building land	*2.97*	*3.59*	*3.10*	3.44	*2.82*	*3.56*	*3.09*	*3.65*	*2.94*	*3.56*
Affordability of living	*2.48*	4.11	3.21	3.97	*2.30*	4.24	*3.06*	4.30	*2.60*	4.17
Career opportunities	3.74	4.25	3.20	4.28	3.82	4.33	3.92	**4.56**	3.70	4.32
Economic situation	4.01	4.29	3.26	4.03	4.02	4.34	3.98	4.11	3.88	4.25
Quality of living	**4.54**	**4.58**	**4.24**	**4.46**	**4.46**	**4.67**	**4.28**	**4.50**	**4.42**	**4.59**
Reputation of region	3.97	3.74	3.54	*3.41*	4.06	3.74	3.88	3.73	3.90	3.68
Safety	**4.55**	**4.57**	**4.30**	**4.29**	4.31	**4.60**	3.98	**4.43**	**4.34**	**4.52**

Note. The three categories with the highest satisfaction are highlighted in **bold**, whereas the three categories with the lowest satisfaction are highlighted in *italics* (for the current as well as for the desired situation)

Table 2 Satisfaction with the general legislation, taxation law, family law, and civil law (country of residence)

	Germany	Austria	Switzerland	Liechtenstein
General legislation	3.40	3.56	3.81	3.77
Taxation law	2.62	3.66	3.34	3.82
Family law	3.41	3.42	3.42	3.64
Civil law	3.27	3.52	3.50	3.67

Table 3 Satisfaction of the general legislation, labor law, taxation law, and business law (country of workplace)

	Germany	Austria	Switzerland	Liechtenstein
General legislation	3.40	3.63	3.85	3.74
Labor law	3.34	3.47	3.34	3.76
Taxation law	2.92	3.19	3.42	3.72
Business law	3.37	3.50	3.50	3.74

5 Discussion and Conclusion

5.1 Liechtenstein

In order to draw a final conclusion and answer the question why people are currently living in the Lake Constance-Alpine Rhine Valley and where they see potential to improve the region's attractiveness, the study compared the results from different questions with the same items. This should help to gain insights on how the region can strengthen its reputation and remain competitive in the future and reveal the topics which should be tackled first. First, a comparison of the current satisfaction and the importance of several site selection factors were carried out. The satisfaction and the importance of several factors for the choice of a new occupation were compared. The study showed that there are certain topics where the difference between the current and the ideal situation is bigger compared with others. Generally, it seems that what is important is already here and in a sufficient manner. Nevertheless, there are certain topics which should be tackled first and which might ensure that the region will maintain its attractiveness. Especially the affordability and accessibility of living space and the improvement of the work-life balance as well as the possibility to change jobs within the region and more space for self-responsibility seem to be promising topics to advance the role of Liechtenstein as a key player in the agglomeration Lake Constance-Alpine Rhine Valley.

To investigate possibilities for further development of the Lake Constance-Alpine Rhine Valley, some general measures were proposed, and the participants had to decide which actions should be realized in order to increase the attractiveness of the region. With 49 votes, the encouragement of job creation and the support for midsize businesses is the number one measure. The second most common action seems to be a stronger attraction of high potentials, followed by the idea that high-tech companies should be supported, as they play an important role as innovators and job creators to the region. A better work-life balance is also highly favored as well as the desire that the region should be more visible in a cross-border manner. As other potential measures seem to be also very attractive for the participants, the distinction between the most liked actions and the others is very slight.

5.2 *Austria*

Based on this research, it can be concluded that the Austrians living in Alpine Rhine Valley value security and the surrounding nature where they live and are very content with the current state of these issues. In addition, the residents of the area value a good work-life balance which they both perceive and prefer to be tipped a little more toward work than their personal lives.

Overall, the people are content with their current work-life balance and the support they are provided toward this. This can also be seen when asked about the future of the Rhine Valley area and how to develop it; the most popular answers were centered around providing better work opportunities and improving the surrounding infrastructure. Therefore, the outcome that the natural environment is of huge importance for the residents of the region was not surprising. This phenomenon occurs because the Alpine Rhine Valley is well known for its unique landscape with the Alps, mountains, and valleys. Regarding work-life balance, 41% perceive a 50-50 work-life balance; the remaining people tend more to the "work side" rather than to enlarge their "life side." This could be a cultural reason, as people from Vorarlberg are known as busy, hard workers in order to reach their goals. Additionally, people could need to work more, as they have difficulties to afford their living standards. Moreover, the result of disposing a considerable high number of knowledge workers who are in a high hierarchical position in the Alpine Rhine region was also unexpected, as nearly the majority (46%) of the interviewees counts to this group. The need for highly qualified employees in a highly service sector-oriented economy in which companies have to differentiate themselves from their competitors and the great access to universities and other educational centers are possible reasons for the high percentage of knowledge workers.

5.3 *Switzerland*

The paper showed that the residents of the Swiss part of the Alpine Rhine Valley are satisfied with their place. Even if most of them live there because it is their place of birth or due to their family and friends, they appreciate the high quality of living. Moreover, the results of the survey showed that work-life balance is very important for the inhabitants of the Alpine Rhine Valley. It is obvious that work overloading is common, so it would be inaccurate to say that people put less effort into their job to earn higher wages. There are also some other factors that are important for them as well. The participants seem to be satisfied with the working conditions. Moreover, not only the high salaries are the reason for this satisfaction but also the good tax system and law regulations that play a significant role. Furthermore, an important aspect of working conditions is the distance between the home and the job location. The survey showed that it takes people at least 15 minutes by car to get from their house to their work locations. Additionally, 60% of the participants have their own car. These results highlight that workers are looking for more comfort and convenience by using their car. The inhabitants of the Swiss Alpine Rhine Valley are satisfied with the quality of living there. They especially appreciate the landscape and the safety. As already mentioned, the participants consider the work-life balance in the Alpine Rhine Valley satisfying. Most of them want a 50-50 work-life balance. Nearly none of them want to work less than 50% of their time. The participants hope the region will develop to create more job opportunities, improve education, and get better infrastructure.

It is safe to say that the Alpine Rhine Valley in Switzerland is currently attractive for its inhabitants. They also see advantages in the living aspect as well as in their jobs. In summary, the people are happy with their current work-life balance. Nevertheless, there are still some improvements they are looking forward to.

5.4 Germany

When considering all results in relation to Germany, there are some aspects which attract attention. When analyzing the satisfaction of the surveyed interviewees, the factors with the lowest values were still not negative and above neutral, and therefore always rather positive. This shows that the overall satisfaction in the studied region is very positive, and there are only minor factors which tend to be negative. This might also be related to the fact that people in this area are very close to their families and therefore are more satisfied. Another important finding is that there are major differences between the generations in regard to their work-life balance and future plans of life. Another very important finding shows the influence of the neighboring countries, which leads to a decreasing satisfaction because of better conditions in the bordering countries. Also, the future of the region is perceived as very positive among the participants. They wish for development toward a more high-tech oriented and internationally important region in order to attract new talents and provide a political, economic, as well as a stable and sustainable environment. Furthermore, there is the desire for further development in the areas of infrastructure and the healthcare systems.

The participants see a very high potential for the Lake Constance-Alpine Rhine Valley region to attract talents and high potentials. They would like to have a more balanced work-life, to present the Alpine Rhine Valley region politically, higher visibility for international business, and support for high-tech companies and innovative companies which might help as technological and economical accelerators.

Also, improvements in infrastructure and health system and cooperation between companies and educational institutions are among the top desired changes within the survey. People throughout all generations perceive the importance to improve in different fields (e.g., infrastructure, health system, support for talents/high potentials, higher visibility and interconnectedness) equally.

5.5 Limitations

One problem that occurred during the research project was that the dropout rate of 25% was pretty high. This could be either attributed to the excess length of the questionnaire or to ambiguous questions and terms such as "Lake Constance-Alpine Rhine Valley region" or "work-life balance." Moreover, respondents from Germany and Switzerland are slightly underrepresented in the sample. Due to the fact that the questionnaire was only conducted in the agglomeration area "Lake Constance-Alpine Rhine Valley," the results are only valid for this region. It is suggested to have a bigger sample for further investigations as there still might be some deviations regarding survey answers. The respondents do not have the urge to improve family friendliness, cultural activities, or lawful equality. That might have to do with the fact that economic measures have a much higher priority, and it is not among the essential factors when considering the future outlooks.

5.6 Future Developments

The interviewees were asked to give suggestions in order to enhance future attractiveness of the Lake Constance-Alpine Rhine Valley region. This issue is analyzed by identifying the five factors in each country that were most frequently chosen from respondents. In general, a lot of similarities of the responses among the countries could be found.

In all four countries, respondents found that high-tech companies as the "number one innovator" should be increasingly encouraged. In Austria, 54% of respondents chose this measure, in Switzerland 51%, in Germany 40%, and in Liechtenstein 40%. Also, higher investments in infrastructure ranked in the top 5 in three countries. This is surprising since the transportation network tends to be highly developed in Central European countries, for example, in Austria (Siegl 2015). The term "infrastructure" may be too vague, which leaves a lot of room for interpretation for respondents (like, e.g., "infrastructure" as referring to public transportation only). Nevertheless, in Austria, 47% of respondents consider this measure as being important, in Switzerland 46%, and in Germany 44%. Moreover, respondents in Austria (46%), Germany (44%), and Liechtenstein (42%) argue for focusing on attracting and binding talents and high potentials to the region. In three countries, respondents suggest improving the work-life balance. In Switzerland, 51% chose this measure, in Germany 47%, and in Liechtenstein 41%. To sum up, respondents in all countries agreed on the fact that in the future, measures with regard to high-tech companies, infrastructure, talents, high potentials, and work-life balance should be taken.

However, the responses also differ among the countries in some way. For example, whereas in Germany and Switzerland respondents did not consider support for SMEs to be an important measure, it was highly ranked in Austria (52%) and Liechtenstein (42%). Moreover, increased cooperation between universities and businesses was mainly chosen in Austria (49%) and Switzerland (43%). In Germany and Switzerland, the respondents argued for improvements in free time activities with 49% and 44%. This did not seem to be of high importance in the other two countries. In conclusion, since SMEs highly contribute to the economic output in Europe, such as in Austria (Siegl 2015), it seems most surprising that measures regarding SMEs were not ranked higher in Germany and Switzerland.

5.7 Concluding Remarks

In conclusion, a lot of similarities of the responses among the countries could be found. However, the responses also differ among the countries in some way. With regard to the working situation, respondents in all countries indicated that they were most satisfied with the working environment and success they have in their job. In contrast to this, the respondents were most dissatisfied with their wages and work-life balance in Austria and Germany and the possibility to change jobs and have opportunity for advancement in Liechtenstein and Switzerland. When looking for a new job, respondents among all countries agreed that job security is the most important factor. With regard to the legal situation, it could be mentioned that if you have a higher standard of living, it seems that the people are more satisfied with the legal system. However, the legal system in Liechtenstein seemed to provide the best conditions in comparison with the other three countries. When it comes to work-life balance, respondents in all countries indicated that they want to spend less time at work and more time at home. Nevertheless, respondents seemed to be satisfied with their current work-life balance situation. Regarding the attractiveness of the region, respondents indicated that the most important factors why they live there are family and friends, being born there, safety, and career opportunities. Moreover, respondents seemed to be most satisfied with nature and scenery, safety, and general living standard. However, they are most dissatisfied with available properties and affordable living. In all countries, respondents agreed that in the future, measures with regard to high-tech companies, infrastructure, talents, high potentials, and work-life balance should be taken.

This leads us to the following answers for our two research questions:

The most important factors of why people live in the Lake Constance-Alpine Rhine Valley region are proximity to (i) family and friends, (ii) safety, (iii) good career opportunities, and (iv) high standard of living.

However, people expressed dissatisfaction with affordable living and availability of property in the region, and it takes at least 1 hour to find recreational facilities such as department stores, theaters, or diverse restaurants. The transportation system is expensive and is uncomfortable for longer journeys. Furthermore, the participants are concerned about the cross-border cooperation between the education sectors. Even worse, they experience a lack of job opportunities, especially in the high-tech industries. At the moment, there are too few knowledge-based companies in the Alpine Rhine Valley. All of the four countries provide similar conditions regarding these factors. Thus, Liechtenstein should focus on attracting international high-tech companies, as well as talents and high potentials, to the country in order to strengthen its competitive position in the agglomeration area.

References

Arribas-Bel D, Sanz-Gracia F (2014) The validity of the monocentric city model in a polycentric age: US metropolitan areas in 1990, 2000 and 2010. Urban Geogr 35(7):980–997

BBSR (2011) Metropolitan areas in Europe. Retrieved from Bonn http://www.inta-aivn.org/images/cc/Metropolisation/background%20documents/Metropolitan_Europe_BBSR_Study.pdf

Brown J, Chapain C, Murie A, Lutz J, Gibney J, Barber A (2008) Birmingham: towards a creative knowledge economy? Understanding the attractiveness of the metropolitan region for creative knowledge workers (9075246684). http://acre.socsci.uva.nl/results/documents/wp5.3_birmingham.pdf

Capello R, Fratesi U, Resmini L (2011) Regional attractiveness and its determinants. In: Capello R, Fratesi U, Resmini L (eds) Globalization and regional growth in Europe: past trends and future scenario. Springer, Heidelberg, pp 191–213

Carrillo FJ, Yigitcanlar T, Baum S, Horton S (2007) Attracting and retaining knowledge workers in knowledge cities. J Knowl Manag 11:6

Florida R (2002) The rise of the creative class, vol 9, 2nd edn. Basic Books, New York

Frenkel A, Bendit E, Kaplan S (2013) Residential location choice of knowledge-workers: the role of amenities, workplace and lifestyle. Cities 35:33–41

Güldenberg S, Hecker L, Klammer A, Wilhelm S, Schurr FA, Staub PA (2017) Residential choice in polycentric border-crossing agglomeration areas: the example of the Lake Constance-Alpine Rhine Valley. Int J Knowl Based Dev 8(4):367–387

Güldenberg S, Ernst E, North K (2021) Managing work in the digital economy – challenges, strategies and practices for the next decade. Springer, Berlin

Hunnius Y (2015) So findet jedes Unternehmen seine Talente. Denkraum 2:12–13

Jirásková E, Žižka M (2011) The significance of business localization factors in the Czech Republic. Creative Knowl Soc 1(2):16–36

Kloosterman RC, Lambregts B (2001) Clustering of economic activities in polycentric urban regions: the case of the Randstad. Urban Stud 38(4):717–732

Kloosterman RC, Musterd S (2001) The polycentric urban region: towards a research agenda. Urban Stud 38(4):623–633

Kuehn M (2016) Peripherisierung und Stadt: Städtische Planungspolitiken gegen den Abstieg. Transcript Verlag, Bielefeld, Germany

Laulajainen R, Stafford HA (2013) Corporate geography: business location principles and cases, vol 31. Springer, Dordrecht, The Netherlands

Meijers E, Hoogerbrugge M, Hollander K (2012) A strategic knowledge and research agenda on polycentric metropolitan areas. http://www.platform31.nl/uploads/media_item/media_item/23/1/KRA_Polycentric_metropolitan_areas-1398346137.pdf
North K, Güldenberg S (2011) Effective knowledge work: answers to the management challenge of the 21st century. Emerald Group Publishing, Bingley, UK
Obkircher S (2011) Das Alpenrheintal im Wandel: Besonderheiten der Region, Grenzerfahrungen und regionale Identitäten im Generationenvergleich, vol 9. Roderer Verlag, Regensburg
OECD (2016) Regional development. http://www.oecd.org/gov/regional-policy/regionaldevelopment.htm
Ogawa H, Fujita M (1980) Equilibrium land use patterns in a nonmonocentric city. J Reg Sci 20(4):455–475
Oueslati W, Alvanides S, Garrod G (2015) Determinants of urban sprawl in European cities. Urban Stud 52(9):1594–1614
Płaziak M, Szymańska AI (2014) Role of modern factors in the process of choosing a location of an enterprise. Procedia Soc Behav Sci 120:72–83
Scharting J, Saurwein K, Oberkircher S, Coy M (2008) Aspekte nachhaltiger Regionalentwicklung im Grenzraum Alpenrheintal, Konzeption eines Forschungsprojektes und erste Ergebnisse. https://www.uibk.ac.at/geographie/igg/berichte/2010/pdf/alpenrhein.pdf
Schlegel H (2009) Grenzfälle, Grenzgänge, Grenzländer. Hochpaterre, pp 16–17. Retrieved from http://renat.li/z_Gemeinsam%20denken,%20eigenst%C3%A4ndig%20umsetzen.pdf
Siegl R (2015) Österreich - Eröffnet neue Perspektiven für Ihr Unternehmen. In: Ö. Ansieldungsberater (ed)
Sieverts T (2012) Zwischenstadt: zwischen Ort und Welt, Raum und Zeit, Stadt und Land, vol 118. Vieweg+Teubner Verlag, Wiesbaden, Germany
Simon S, Wyssen T (2011) Praxisleitfaden Wirtschaftsstandort Alpenrheintal: Optimierung der Arbeitsortattraktivität für Fach- und Führungskräfte. Retrieved from Chur, Switzerland http://www.htwchur.ch/uploads/media/LeitfadenAlpenrheintal.pdf
Statistikplattform Bodensee (2021) The International Lake Constance Region in Figures 2021. https://www.statistik-bodensee.org/files/downloads/publikationen/Die%20internationale%20Bodenseeregion%20in%20Zahlen/Die%20internationale%20Bodenseeregion%20in%20Zahlen%202021/TRA_StatistikLepo_2021_EN_WEB_gesamt.pdf
Staub P, Gasser R, Kaps V, Martinez C (2014) Kreativwirtschaftsbericht für das Fürstentum Liechtenstein. Retrieved from Vaduz, Liechtenstein. www.uni.li/Portals/0/docs/ar/forschung/PARK/UNI_Kreativwirtschaftsbericht_02.12.2014_Web.pdf
Wheaton WC (2004) Commuting, congestion, and employment dispersal in cities with mixed land use. J Urban Econ 55(3):417–438
Yigitcanlar T, Baum S, Horton S (2007) Attracting and retaining knowledge workers in knowledge cities. J Knowl Manag 11:6–17

Cross-Border Philanthropy: Current Challenges in Corporate Governance and Financial Risk Management

Francesco A. Schurr and Marco J. Menichetti

Abstract Philanthropy has gained more importance around the globe. Foundations are one of the most chosen organizational forms to pursue philanthropic interests. Legal systems around the world are competing to offer the best legal environment to their foundation. The authors will analyze how Liechtenstein's new provisions in foundation law, which offers every foundation to tailor its governance structure to fit its founders' demands, make the small state an ideal and neutral location for the realization of international philanthropic projects. In the second part, the focus shifts to the financial challenges and risks foundations must face and how to manage them. As foundations in most cases miss the in-house knowledge to manage these risks, they behave more risk-averse than necessary. Together with the framework of risk-averse financial market authorities, financial advantages of a professional risk and asset management approach remain on average unused.

1 Corporate Governance Considerations for Cross-Border Philanthropy

1.1 Introduction

In recent years, there has been tremendous growth in philanthropy around the world. In order to enable such charitable giving, legal entities have been used in order to structure the transfer of wealth. Foundations, in particular, have become increasingly popular for such purposes. This, in turn, has led to greater competition among various jurisdictions especially with regard to the civil law rules and other

F. A. Schurr (✉)
University of Innsbruck, Innsbruck, Austria
e-mail: francesco.schurr@uibk.ac.at

M. J. Menichetti
Liechtenstein Business School, University of Liechtenstein, Vaduz, Liechtenstein
e-mail: marco.menichetti@uni.li

P. Droege et al. (eds.), *Cross-Border Life and Work*, Contributions to Management Science, https://doi.org/10.1007/978-3-031-34362-9_3

provisions regarding foundation governance. In order to achieve an optimal governance structure, Liechtenstein has struck a balance between the range of mechanisms available and its legal system providing a number of attractive options for cross-border philanthropic foundations.

1.2 Philanthropic Foundations and Jurisdictional Competition

Foundations are currently experiencing great popularity across the world for a number of different social and economic reasons (Schurr 2011, p. 159). The rise of philanthropic foundations, referred to as common-benefit foundations in Liechtenstein, is due to the effects of the current financial situation, which has led to spending cuts in many state-sponsored areas, such as culture and science.

In order to choose the ideal location for a common-benefit foundation, individuals must take various factors into account. In this regard, they will typically take professional advice based on a set of criteria, taking into account tax considerations, the degree of legal flexibility available with regard to the foundation's purpose, and, increasingly, issues concerning foundation governance (Schurr 2014).

In Europe, a foundation is an entity holding ownerless assets. It is the founder's will, which is set out upon formation of the foundation, which determines the purpose and structure of the foundation (Ekkehard et al. 2008). Due to the lack of a corporate element, foundations are considerably more susceptible to abuse than any other legal entities. Therefore, a careful balance must be struck between administration and supervision in order to ensure compliance with the foundation's purpose.

The following factors play a major role in decisions regarding location:

- A high degree of legal certainty over a long period of time
- The greatest degree of freedom possible in establishing the internal organization of the foundation
- Confidentiality concerning the formation of the foundation
- A high degree of expertise among the official authorities and courts involved

These factors highlight the inextricable connection between a foundation's governance and its purpose.

Within the EU (and also the EEA), competition among jurisdictions has been stimulated through the ECJ's case law the basic freedoms, in particular on the free movement of capital [1] and the law on the freedom of establishment. [2] Therefore, a prospective founder may now freely choose to establish a foundation in any of the EEA legal systems recognizing foundations. It is therefore likely that such jurisdictions will tailor their (tax and civil law) legislation in order to attract business in this sector. Liechtenstein, for example, reformed its foundation law to align with

[1] Case C-384/06 Stauffer [2006] ECR I-08203; Case C-318/07 Persche [2009] ECR I-359.

[2] Case C-212/97 Centros [1999] ECR I-1459; Case C-208/00 Überseering [2002] ECR I-9919.

contemporary standards and requirements. [3] The new provisions (Art. 552 §§ 1ff) entered into force on April 1, 2009, and provide an ideal basis to attract prospective founders.

1.3 Governance

1.3.1 Corporate Governance

Foundation governance represents a development of the issue of corporate governance, which is a term originating from the academic study of business. Corporate governance is important to ensure that companies are protected from misconduct by its management bodies, as hard law is often not a sufficient means to deal with complex business management situations. This is especially true in the so-called principal-agent relationship (Kreutz 2007, p. 51), where numerous corporate governance codes have been drafted and published, setting out good management practice and internal corporate control mechanisms. These codes are normally followed on a voluntary basis using the "comply-or-explain" principle (Werder 2003, p. 83; Jakob 2008, p. 15). Their use leads to a standardization of business management standards, and their monitoring or demonstrating harmonization may also be achieved through soft laws (Hopt 2003, p. 32).

1.3.2 Foundation Governance Models

Unlike companies and many other types of legal entity, foundations do not have a corporate element, such as having members or shareholders. Instead, it is a special purpose fund which owns itself and whose purpose is central to its existence (Schurr 2011, p. 161). Due to its nature, an organizational structure suited to the long-term pursuit of the foundation's purpose is required (Schauer 2008, p. 28). Furthermore, stricter control mechanisms are required than in corporate governance (Müller and Fischer 2009, p. 114), but these should not prevent the purpose from being realized. A fine balance therefore must be maintained.

In Europe, there are different models of supervision. In some jurisdictions, the task of supervision is assigned to public institutions: for example, public administrative bodies in Germany (Richter 2007, p. 789) and courts in Austria (Briem 2009, p. 14), where beneficiaries' rights ensure effective supervision (Kalss 2008, p. 50). The model in Liechtenstein is a combination of the two models mentioned above. It

[3] See the Law of June 26, 2008, on the Amendment of the Persons and Companies Act, Liechtenstein Law Gazette 2008, No. 220 (Gesetz vom 26.06.2008 über die Abänderung des Personen- und Gesellschaftsrechts, LGBl. 2008, Nr. 220); in this context, see Schauer, M. (2008); with regard to its historical development, see Tschütscher, K. (2008). Das neue liechtensteinische Stiftungsrecht–Entstehungsgeschichte und Gesamtüberblick. *LJZ*, 4, 79.

distinguishes between common-benefit foundations and private-benefit foundations. The former is subject to state supervision, while the latter is supervised by courts acting upon petitions (Kerres and Proell 2009, p. 322).

1.3.3 Foundation Governance as Soft Law

As with legal entities, there is a development toward foundations regulating themselves (Jakob 2009, para. 444). In order to overcome any lacunae in hard law, soft law measures are required, meaning that voluntary foundations' governance codes, such as the Swiss Foundation Code, are being drafted (Sprecher et al. 2009). While these codes are voluntary, their importance should not be underestimated. In the past, such self-regulatory standards have significantly influenced hard law, as Liechtenstein being an example of this.

1.4 Liechtenstein Foundation Law: Structures of Governance

1.4.1 Internal and External Governance

The recent reform of Liechtenstein foundation law means that statutory law has been optimized for governance structures. In order to enable further adaptation by founders, many of the provisions are optional.

Liechtenstein foundation law now has a combination of external and internal governance, which provides for two different legal instruments: common- and private-benefit foundations (Art 552 §§ 1ff PGR). Under these provisions, common-benefit foundations, which include philanthropic foundations, are supervised by the Foundation Supervision Authority (STIFA). Note however that while these beneficiaries are entitled to numerous supervisory rights in relation to private-benefit foundations under Art. 552 § 9 PGR, these rights are retracted under Art. 552 § 12 PGR where a foundation is placed under the supervision of STIFA.

1.4.2 The Definition of Common Benefit

Pursuant to Art. 552 § 29(1) PGR, the STIFA is responsible for supervising common-benefit foundations. A foundation is defined as a common-benefit foundation if its purpose is of benefit to the general public, which it is considered to be if a foundation's activity serves the common good in a charitable, religious, humanitarian, scientific, cultural, moral, social, sporting, or ecological sense (Art. 107(4a) PGR). A special feature in Liechtenstein that is also worth noting is that serving the common good also encompasses cases where the benefit of the foundation's activity is restricted to a particular category of people (H.S.H. Prince Michael of Liechtenstein 2008). In comparison with other jurisdictions, the Liechtenstein definition of common-benefit for the purposes of determining the relevant governance structure is liberal, especially as the principle of private autonomy even allows the founder to pursue common-benefit goals without authorization by the foundation's management. Where such goals are in line with the common good, they will be regarded as pursuing a common benefit (Hopt and Reuter 2001, p. 10).

1.4.3 Official Supervision of Common-Benefit Foundations

In order to ensure STIFA's political independence, there is cooperation with the courts where punitive measures are required. In addition, responsibility for foundation supervision was transferred to the GBOERA (the Office of Land and Public Registration) (Art. 552 § 29(2) PGR) as part of the foundation law reform, making STIFA independent of the government. With regard to STIFA's duties and responsibilities under the new Liechtenstein foundation law, it is necessary to draw a distinction between areas requiring preventative and punitive measures.

Preventative Measures

The scope of the preventative measures available is governed by the second sentence of Art. 552 § 29(3). It permits the STIFA to require a foundation to provide information and to order an inspection of a foundation's books and documents, a task which an audit authority must carry out (Jakob 2009, para. 460). Where there are sufficient financial reasons, it is possible to refrain from appointing an audit authority (Art. 552 § 27(5) PGR together with Arts. 4 and 5 of the Regulation of Foundations Act). [4] In such cases, a foundation's books and documents may be inspected by the STIFA (Schurr 2014, p. 181).

Punitive Measures

The scope of the punitive measures available is set out in the fourth sentence of Art. 552 § 29(3) PGR. It empowers the STIFA to ensure, where it is in the best interests of a foundation, that executive bodies are dismissed, resolutions passed by the executive bodies are set aside, or special audits are carried out. STIFA is, however, not permitted to take such measures. It must, instead, file an appropriate petition in court (Schurr 2011, p. 170). By combining two models, Liechtenstein has therefore introduced a so-called supervision of the supervisors: the Swiss model of ongoing state supervision has been merged with the Austrian one, providing supervision by the courts acting only on the basis of petitions (Jakob 2009, para. 461).

[4] Administration, L. N. "Instruction sheet concerning the exemption from the audit office requirement for charitable foundations subject to supervision pursuant to Art 552 § 27 para. 5 PGR in conjunction with Art 5 and Art 6 para. 2 b StRV." Available at: www.llv.li/llv-gboera-home.htm

It remains uncertain whether this double layer of state and court supervision is viable in the long run and perhaps even serves as a model for other European jurisdictions. There are concerns that it leads to an increase in bureaucratic work and expenditure. The ultimate justification is that this sophisticated system of justice can completely eliminate any abuse, leading to greater trust and confidence in it. In respect of the current competition among jurisdictions for cross-border foundation business, a dual system of supervision could become an essential criterion for ensuring that Liechtenstein, rather than another jurisdiction, is chosen (Schurr 2014, p. 182).

Internal and External Governance Combined for Common-Benefit Foundations

For the internal governance of common-benefit foundations in Liechtenstein, an audit authority within the meaning of Art. 552 § 27 PGR must be established, to whom some of the STIFA's duties and responsibilities are delegated. In this respect, the approaches taken by Liechtenstein, Switzerland, and Austria (Arts. 83b, 83c, 87 1bis ZGB, and § 20(3) PSG) have similarities. Upon recommendation by the founder concerned, the appointment of an audit authority is made by the courts (Art. 552 § 27(3) PGR). It is necessary to consider the potential for any obvious conflicts of interest (especially of holding multiple posts in the foundation; Art. 552 § 27(2) PGR) when such appointments are made. A conflict of interest is clearly present in cases where members of another executive body of the foundation, employees of the foundation, any people with close family connections with members of executive bodies of the foundation, and beneficiaries of the foundation are involved (Jakob 2009, para. 390).

Summary

In respect to common-benefit foundations in Liechtenstein, there is cooperation between the STIFA and audit authorities where preventative measures are concerned. Punitive measures are achieved through work by the STIFA together with the courts. The latter is a new approach, which is referred to by the Liechtenstein legislature itself as a key provision of the new system (Landtag des Fürstentums Liechtenstein 2008, p. 111).

1.4.4 Amending the Purpose as a Measure of Governance Structures

Ensuring effective, long-term foundation management may require an amendment to a foundation's purpose. If either the purpose has become unachievable, impermissible, or irrational or the circumstances have changed to the extent that the purpose has acquired a quite different significance or effect, the STIFA may apply for to the court an amendment of the purpose pursuant to Art. 552 § 33 PGR (Schurr

2014, p. 182). This is to prevent a foundation from becoming independent of its founder's intention. Any amendment made for this purpose, must be consistent with the presumed intention of the founder concerned (Rick 2009, paras. 14). If the STIFA does not make such an application for amendment, the foundation participants may, pursuant to Art. 552 § 33(3) PGR, petition the court to amend the purpose (Rick 2009, para. 19).

Under Art. 552 § 34(1) PGR and § 34(2) PGR, respectively, STIFA and foundation participants may also file a petition requesting other contents of a foundation deed or a supplementary foundation deed to be amended (F. Schurr and Büchel 2009, p. 115). Founders, entitled beneficiaries, prospective beneficiaries, discretionary beneficiaries, ultimate beneficiaries, the executive bodies of foundations, and members of these executive bodies are deemed by Art. 552 § 3 PGR to be foundation participants. Due to their exclusion in the definition in Art. 552 § 3 PGR, subsequent donors are not automatically considered to be foundation participants, and it is ultimately for the courts to decide whether they also have locus standi to file petitions as provided for in Art. 552 § 29(4) or Art. 552 § 35(1) PGR (Jakob 2009, para. 468).

1.5 Conclusion

In introducing new provisions on foundation governance, Liechtenstein has taken a highly nuanced approach. The new Liechtenstein foundation law now offers an option enabling every foundation to tailor its governance structure according to its founder's personal demands. The involvement of the courts, particularly where punitive measures are concerned, considerably improves the mandatory supervision of common-benefit foundations by STIFA. A foundation's ability to act entirely autonomously is ultimately protected by the independence of the judiciary, because court involvement in this process prevents the government from exercising any political influence on the work of a foundation via STIFA. For the purposes of realizing international philanthropic projects, this makes Liechtenstein an ideal and neutral location. However, this system has a drawback: it leads to an increase in bureaucracy, which is reduced to a minimum through the involvement of beneficiaries of common-benefit foundations as controlling bodies. Beneficiaries may be granted a right to supervise in cases where the STIFA does not fulfill its supervisory duties and responsibilities (Schurr 2014, p. 190).

The fact that important supervisory powers have been placed in the competence of an audit authority as an internal governance body in relation to common-benefit foundations should be welcomed. It is able to exercise its supervisory functions with more efficiency and less bureaucracy due to its proximity to a foundation council (Schurr 2014, p. 190).

The multilayered approach to the individual supervisory institutions is the main benefit provided by the new governance system under Liechtenstein law (Schurr 2011, p. 171). The implementation of the new foundation law initially caused some confusion; however, the ensuing uncertainty should not be overestimated, and the positive merits of the new provisions must be taken into consideration.

Due to its multidimensional nature, the system of governance established in Liechtenstein adds to its competitiveness in comparison with other European jurisdictions. The heavily administrative-oriented foundation supervisory system relied on by Germany and Switzerland and the heavily court-oriented one relied on by Austria are combined in Liechtenstein's system to create the best of both worlds. The new and innovative tools of foundation governance represent a groundbreaking development in Europe. Consequently, founders wishing to pursue common-benefit purposes will find that Liechtenstein provides an ideal setting.

2 Financial Risks in Cross-Border Philanthropic Institutions

As already mentioned in the first part of this text, there has been a tremendous growth in cross-border philanthropy around the world. This explosive growth went along with a sound analysis and detailed development of legal aspects in connection with philanthropic giving and the legal structure of wealth transfer. In the meantime, strong competition between philanthropic hubs worldwide evolved in order to offer philanthropic individuals an optimal legal framework for their giving. Philanthropic hubs try to attract as many philanthropic institutions as possible, in order to attract at least part of the value-added chain to their domicile. The more of the chain processed within the domicile, the higher the contribution of the philanthropic sector to gross domestic product.

In the existing literature, the financial tasks of philanthropic institutions are more or less completely neglected. If we understand the philanthropic sector as working in a strongly competitive environment, financial aims and duties of philanthropic institutions cannot be neglected. As philanthropic institutions try to proof the impact of their common-benefit work, they need a professionally working finance department and treasury. An optimized corporate governance should go hand in hand with optimized financial processes.

Within this chapter, we will in a first step try to structure a general business model of a cross-border philanthropic institution, then identify their financial risks, and finally give a short overview on how to manage these financial risks. In a final section, specific challenges related with asset management issues will be singled out.

2.1 General Business Model of Philanthropic Institutions

The business model of philanthropic institutions is dependent on founders' decisions on a common-benefit status and on his capital donation, on philanthropic institutions' governing bodies, and on projects to be supported by the institution.

Individuals and companies could act as founders of philanthropic institutions. The constitutional decision is the choice of the domicile and legal structure in order to optimally realize the founder's intention. The founder decides on the common-benefit goal of the institution. The business model of a philanthropic institution faces important challenges described in Fig. 1. The aim of such an institution is supporting specific projects, which correlate to the given common-benefit goal. Based on a capital donation of the founder, a philanthropic institution is investing financial means and receives resultant cash flow income. Most domiciles prohibit philanthropic institutions to support projects by using the initial capital donation. This underlines the importance of earnings based on the invested donation for fulfilling the purpose of a philanthropic institution. In case financial risks are not accurately managed or the asset allocation decisions do not result in investments earnings, a philanthropic institution cannot support common-benefit projects any more. In such a case, the founder or third parties could transfer additional funds (after inception) in order to make the philanthropic institution capable of acting.

The donation is placed in a specific currency, but for sound asset allocation reasons, this donation should be invested according to an appropriate international asset allocation, considering liquidity requirements (Solnik and McLeavey 2009). Asset allocation means investment of donated capital to cash instruments, bonds, stocks, and alternative investments (Bodie et al. 2014). Investment earnings could be volatile over time because of volatility of stock, commodity, and bond prices as well as exchange rates. The constitutional aim of a philanthropic institution is to

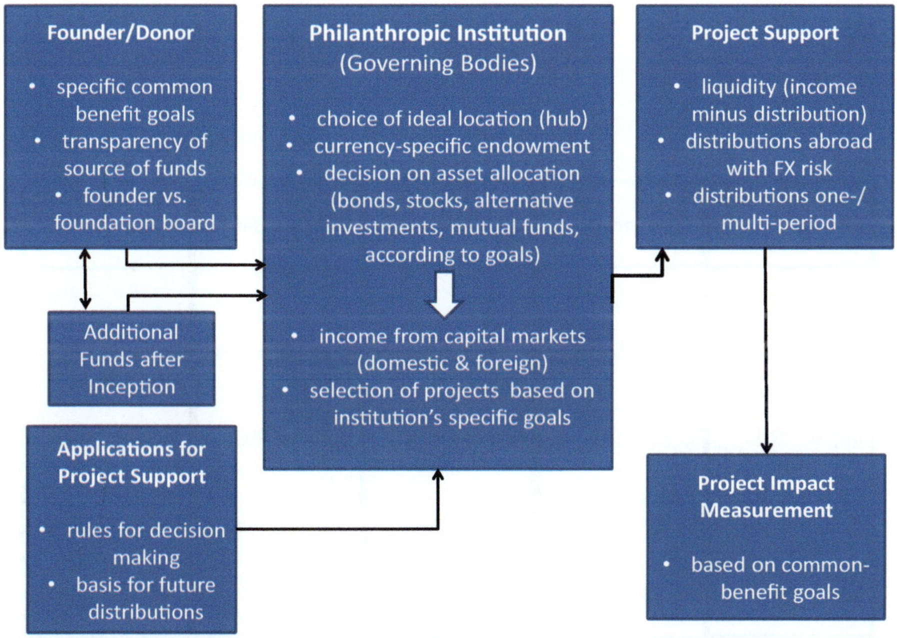

Fig. 1 Business model of philanthropic institutions

generate investment earnings in order to support common-benefit projects in compliance with founder's will.

Supported projects could be domestic or abroad and could involve domestic and/or international payments. Supporting decisions of the institution could result in enforceable claims for one or more/multiple periods. Appreciations and depreciations of the foreign currency will make distributions in foreign currency more expensive or cheap. Thus, the liquidity of a philanthropic institution is at risk. The institution could become illiquid, if payments for project supports would exceed investment earnings.

Finally, philanthropic institutions in general want to delineate their contribution to societal problem solutions. Thus, they often want to measure the impact resulting from their common-benefit work.

2.2 *Financial Risks and Management Approaches*

2.2.1 Overview on Financial Risks

Based on the explanation of philanthropic institutions' business model in the previous section, we group resulting financial risks into the following major risk categories, shown in Fig. 2:

- External risks
- Fixed-income risks
- Equity risks
- Cross-border risks
- Operational risks

External	Fixed-Income	Equity	Cross-Border	Operational
Reputational Risk	Diversification Risk	Diversification Risk	Exchange Rate Risk	Source of Funds Risk
Impact Risk	Credit Risk	Market Risk	Political Risk	Risk of Capital Preservation
Cultural Risk	Interest Rate Risk	Firm-Specific Risk	Transfer Risk	Liquidity Risk

Fig. 2 Financial risks of philanthropic institutions

2.2.2 Risk Management Approaches

External risks are formed by reputational, impact, and cultural risks. Reputational risk is caused by negative publicity caused by the institution's business practices. As an example, reputational risk is caused by inappropriate investment decisions, criticized by society or founder. Impact risk is the risk of not achieving impact goals according to the philanthropic aims of the institution. Cultural risks arise from different opinions between founder and governing bodies of the philanthropic institution. Cooperation between the governing bodies could suffer from strong obstacles caused by cultural risk.

Management of these external risks has to be classified as a strategic task of the institution. Operational and strategic risks are a major concern of philanthropic institutions. A founder cannot really guarantee with the framework established that such risks are avoided. The governing bodies of the institution are responsible to design and supervise processes that exclude such risk as much as possible. These risks damage the trust in the institution and may lead to a collapse of the philanthropic institution (Zurich 2015; Commission 2012; Kistruck et al. 2013; Sargeant and Shang 2011).

Fixed-income risks consist of diversification, interest rate risk, and credit risk. With diversification, volatility of financial assets can be reduced substantially. Interest rate risk describes price changes of fixed-income investments like bonds in case of changing market interest rates; in case of increasing (decreasing) interest rates on markets, bond prices will fall (increase), resulting in losses (profits) for investors. Change in the creditworthiness or default probability of an indebted person or institution, thus that the borrower will be unable to meet the obligations, is called credit risk.

Diversification can be achieved by introducing an elaborate mix of assets, supported by the use of specific steering instruments. Interest rate risk can be managed by duration and convexity, acting as sensitivities. With duration matching of assets and liabilities, an institution is trying to keep the interest rate risk as low as possible. Credit risk could be managed by structuring financial processes within an organization, such as knowing your customer, analyzing nonfinancial risks, or monitoring, but also by using financial instruments like credit default swaps (Bodie et al. 2014; Gantenbein and Spremann 2014; Hull 2011, 2012; Solnik and McLeavey 2009).

Equity risks consist of diversification, market risks, and firm-specific risks. Market risk, also called systematic risk, is generated by the overall performance of financial markets of an economy; this risk cannot be eliminated by diversification. Firm-specific risks are tied to the performance of individual securities; specific risks can be reduced or even eliminated by diversification.

Often used instruments for measuring market risks are value at risk (VaR) or variance covariance matrix. Market risk could be hedged by using derivatives, like forward, futures, or options. Hedging firm-specific risks can be managed by diversification (Bodie et al. 2014; Hull 2011, 2012; Kistruck et al. 2013; Andersen et al. 2007; Bangia et al. 2002).

Cross-border risks are made up of exchange rate, political, and transfer risk. Changing exchange rates influence values of financial assets as well as the values of investment earnings. Transfer risk means the risk of not being allowed to transfer payments across borders caused by rulings of the local government. Political risks comprise decisions of local governments affecting the business of companies and their financial results. In the case of philanthropic institutions, investment earnings are affected.

Exchange rate risks can be managed operationally by having a view on developing clear and concise processes of risk management, i.e., know your reference currencies. In the long run, strategic decision-making is necessary, international sourcing as being only one of them. Transfer risk and political risk management is the duty of management as well as the supervisory board, based on an ongoing analysis of the political and economic stability of affected countries (Menichetti et al. 2013; Eiteman et al. 2013; Sargeant and Shang 2011; Commission 2012; Sercu 2009).

Operational risks are comprised of source of funds, capital preservation, and liquidity risk. Source of funds risk refers to founder's capital donation and where it comes from. Is this capital donation legally and ethically correct? Groups and associations receiving benefits by philanthropic institutions take care of the source of their funds to avoid any negative publicity for their social and common-benefit project. Another operational risk is capital preservation. Most legal domiciles demand philanthropic institutions to preserve the value of the initial capital donation. Caused by the volatility of capital markets, it is an ongoing duty of the governing body to guarantee value preservation. Liquidity risk arises because of the already mentioned mismatch between investment earnings and project distributions.

Operational risks, too, mainly have to be managed by developing clear and concise processes of risk management. Responsibility has to be located with management and board of directors. An appropriate information tool has to be developed to plan current and future liquidity (Braemer 2015; Commission 2010, 2016).

2.3 *Specific Challenges in Asset Management*

The founder of a philanthropic institution decides on the specific common-benefit goal and equips the institution with a capital donation. Governing bodies of the philanthropic institution will then have to invest the capital. The law is in general not giving any framework on how this capital should be invested.

In most domiciles, governing bodies have to preserve the capital donation. They can even be made liable in case the capital decreases in value. Some domiciles do not know that liability regarding the capital donation. But even in domiciles without that liability, governing bodies behave very risk-averse, as they very much feel responsible for preserving the capital donation of a common-benefit society. Often, the asset allocation decision is assigned to professional asset managers. They, too, work with a high risk-aversion, as this is what they assume their principles want them to do (Kargl and Müller 2015; Maginn et al. 2007).

Investing with a high risk-aversion will lead to an **asset allocation** based on cash and high rated bonds, only a low fraction of stocks or even no stocks. Any other instruments like alternative investments will probably not be used. In periods with high interest rates, philanthropic institutions with such an asset allocation enough will earn capital earnings to be able to support projects. In periods with low or negative interest rates, the philanthropic institution will not earn any investment earning, and thus it will not be capable to support projects any more.

Besides the asset allocation decision, it has to be defined **what securities** to choose. This poses the question, if the decision on sectors and securities could be held independent from the specific aim of the charitable institution. By reason of reputational risk, common-benefit institutions cannot afford to invest in sectors and businesses contradicting to the charitable aim. One possibility would be to invest into socially responsible and sustainable investments (Blanchett 2014; Schumacher 2013).

To summarize, there is more need for research on how to structure risk management in general and specifically the asset allocation decision for charitable institutions and how to implement it by choosing the security selection. Specifically, for philanthropic institutions, we need research on how much risk-taking can be accepted—by the founder and by management bodies of the institution. Research results have to be implemented in publicly available framework by the charity authority. Offering charitable institutions a clear framework on acceptable risk exposure and financial instruments in use, this would significantly reduce the uncertainty for governing bodies in charitable institutions as well as the excessive risk-aversion of all parties involved.

2.4 Conclusion

Charitable institutions are often small entities without a deep professional knowledge in financial management. Thus, management bodies in such institutions are often not aware of risks and challenges they face. Therefore, we have first analyzed financial risks of philanthropic institutions. According to our opinion, financial risks of charitable organizations consist of external risks, fixed-income risks, equity risks, cross-border risks, and operational risks. All these risks contribute to success or collapse of philanthropic institutions, and thus they have to be managed very carefully.

Regarding the asset allocation decision, a clearly defined framework by the responsible authority is necessary. Currently, the existing framework pushes the management bodies of the charitable institution to manage funds in a very risk-averse way that is too conservative. With developing a clear less risk-averse framework by the authority, so far unused asset allocation decisions would be possible to realize. This would improve the investment earnings based on a predefined risk level.

References

Administration LN Instruction sheet concerning the exemption from the audit office requirement for charitable foundations subject to supervision pursuant to Art 552 § 27 para. 5 PGR in conjunction with Art 5 and Art 6 para. 2 b StRV. www.llv.li/llv-gboera-home.htm

Andersen TG, Bollerslev T, Christoffersen P, Diebold FX (2007) Practical volatility and correlation modeling for financial market risk management. In: Carey M, Stulz RM (eds) The risks of financial institutions. University of Chicago Press, Chicago, IL, pp 513–548

Bangia A, Diebold FX, Schuermann T, Stroughair JD (2002) Modeling liquidity risk, with implications for traditional market risk measurement and management. In: Figlewski S, Levich RM (eds) Risk management: the state of the art. Springer, New York, pp 3–13

Blanchett D (2014) Donation risk and optimal endowment portfolio allocations. J Portf Manag 41(1):109–120

Bodie Z, Kane A, Marcus AJ (2014) Investments. McGraw Hill Education, Maidenhead, Berkshire

Braemer C (2015) Philanthropy: the new risk capital? http://ssir.org/articles/entry/philanthropy_the_new_risk_capital. Accessed 5 November 2015

Briem R (2009) Corporate Governance der Privatstiftung unter dem Blickwinkel der aktuellen Judikatur. GesRZ 1:12

Charity Commission (2010) Guidance - charities and risk management (CC26). UK Government Publications. https://www.gov.uk/government/publications/charities-and-risk-management-cc26/charities-and-risk-management-cc26

Charity Commission (2012) Guidance - charity governance, finance and resilience: 15 questions trustees should ask. UK Government Publications. https://www.gov.uk/government/publications/charity-trustee-meetings-15-questions-you-should-ask/charity-trustee-meetings-15-questions-you-should-ask

Charity Commission (2016) Guidance - charity reserves: building resilience. UK Government Publications. https://www.gov.uk/government/publications/charities-and-reserves-cc19/charities-and-reserves

Eiteman DK, Stonehill AI, Moffett MH (2013) Multinational business finance. Pearson Addison-Wesley, Boston, MA

Ekkehard R, Anheier HK, Hopt KJ, Hippel T Vahlpahl T, Then V, et al (2008) Feasibility study on a European foundation statute. Max Planck Institute for Comparative and International Private Law, Centre for Social Investment at the University of Heidelberg. http://ec.europa.eu/internal_market/company/eufoundation/index_en.htm

Gantenbein P, Spremann K (2014) Zinsen, Anleihen, Kredite. De Gruyter Oldenbourg, Munich

H.S.H. Prince Michael of Liechtenstein (2008) Die konkreten Einsatzmöglichkeiten einer gemeinnützigen Stiftung. In: Liechtenstein IH (ed) Das neue liechtensteinische Stiftungsrecht. Schulthess Verlag, Zurich

Hopt KJ (2003) Die rechtlichen Rahmenbedingungen der Corporate Governance. In: Hommelhoff P, Hopt KJ, Werder AV (eds) Handbuch Corporate Governance. Leitung und Überwachung börsennotierter Unternehmen in der Rechts- und Wirtschaftspraxis. Schäffer-Poeschel Verlag, Stuttgart, pp 29–50

Hopt KJ, Reuter D (2001) Stiftungsrecht in Europa: Eine Einführung. In: Hopt KJ, Reuter D (eds) Stiftungsrecht in Europa. Heymann, Cologne

Hull JC (2011) Options futures and other derivatives. Pearson Education, Harlow, UK

Hull J (2012) Risk management and financial institutions. Wiley, Hoboken, NJ

Jakob D (2008) Das neue System der Foundation Governance - Interne und externe Stiftungsaufsicht im neuen liechtensteinischen Stiftungsrecht. Liechtensteinische Juristen-Zeitung 2008:83–89

Jakob D (2009) Die liechtensteinische Stiftung. Liechtenstein-Verlag AG, Vaduz

Kalss S (2008) Grenzen der Einflussnahme von Begünstigten in der Privatstiftung. JEV 48

Kargl S, Müller K (2015) Investment Controlling als Instrument der Risiko-und Haftungsbegrenzung in Stiftungen. Zeitschrift für Stiftungswesen 2015(1):3–6

Kerres C, Proell F (2009) Das neue liechtensteinische Stiftungsrecht. *ecolex* 2009:321–324

Kistruck GM, Qureshi I, Beamish PW (2013) Geographic and product diversification in charitable organizations. J Manag 39(2):496–530
Kreutz M (2007) Verhaltenskodices als wesentliches Element von Corporate-Governance-Systemen in gemeinnützigen Körperschaften. Zeitschrift für Rechtspolitik 40(2):50–54
Landtag des Fürstentums Liechtenstein (2008) Bericht und Antrag der Regierung an den Landtag des Fürstentums Liechtenstein betreffend die Totalrevision des Stiftungsrechts Nr. 13/2008
Maginn JL, Tuttle DL, McLeavey DW, Pinto JE (2007) Managing investment portfolios: a dynamic process. John Wiley & Sons, Hoboken, NJ
Menichetti MJ, Kaiser L, Veress A (2013) The exchange rate dimension in international asset allocation - lessons learned from the current financial crisis. In: Hummel D (ed) The Euro financial crisis: impacts on banking, capital markets, and regulation. Report of the international workshop in Potsdam on July 20/21, 2012. University of Potsdam Press, Potsdam, Germany, pp 85–101
Müller K, Fischer M (2009) Wieviel (Corporate/foundation) governance braucht die Privatstiftung? ZfS 3:112
Richter A (2007) Länderbericht Deutschland. In: Richter A, Wachter T (eds) Handbuch des internationalen Stiftungsrechts. Zerb, Angelbachtal
Rick M (2009) Art 552 §§ 33-35. In: Schauer M, Hammermann B (eds) Kurzkommentar zum liechtensteinischen Stiftungsrecht. Helbing Lichtenhahn, Basel
Sargeant A, Shang J (2011) Growing philanthropy in the United States. A report on the June 2011 Washington, D.C. growing philanthropy summit. Hartsook Institutes for Fundraising, Washington, DC
Schauer M (2008) Grundelemente des neuen liechtensteinischen Stiftungsrechts und die rechtsvergleichende Perspektive. In: Liechtenstein IH (ed) Das neue liechtensteinische Stiftungsrecht. Schulthess Verlag, Zurich
Schumacher I (2013) Die Vermögensverwaltung von Stiftungen schreitet voran, auch beim zweckkonformen Investieren. Das Geld-Magazin 2013:32–34
Schurr FA (2011) Charitable foundations in the Principality of Liechtenstein-tradition and recent developments. Vict Univ Wellingt Law Rev 42:159
Schurr FA (2014) The foundation governance under Liechtenstein foundation law. In: Prele C (ed) Developments in foundation law in Europe. Springer, Dordrecht, pp 175–192
Schurr F, Büchel S (2009) Überlegungen zur Anpassung und Änderung des Stiftungszwecks durch den Stifter bzw ein Organ der Stiftung. Liechtenstein J 110
Sercu P (2009) International finance: theory into practice. Princeton University Press, Princeton, NJ
Solnik BH, McLeavey DW (2009) Global investments. Addison-Wesley Longman, Amsterdam
Sprecher T, Egger P, Janssen M (2009) Swiss Foundation Code 2009 mit Kommentar: Grundsätze und Empfehlungen zur Gründung und Führung von Förderstiftungen (Foundation governance). Helbing Lichtenhahn, Basel
Tschütscher K (2008) Das neue liechtensteinische Stiftungsrecht–Entstehungsgeschichte und Gesamtüberblick. LJZ 4:79
Werder AV (2003) Ökonomische Grundfragen der Corporate Governance. In: Hommelhoff P, Hopt KJ, Werder AV (eds) Handbuch corporate governance–Leitung und Überwachung börsennotierter Unternehmen in der Rechts-und Wirtschaftspraxis. Schäffer-Poeschel Verlag, Stuttgart, pp 3–37
Zurich (2015) Charitytimes – charity risk survey. Zurich. Dublin. http://www.charitytimes.com/digital_editions_eblasts/Zurich_suppliment_digital_edition.pdf

Cross-Border Wealth Management

Martin Angerer, Michael Hanke, Tanja Kirn, Christina Preiner, Martin Wenz, Dirk Zetzsche, and Michael Amann

Abstract Cross-border wealth management is an important topic globally, and particularly relevant in Europe. There is not much literature on drivers of and barriers to this phenomenon. This present article closes this gap and analyzes the economic, legal, and tax drivers of cross-border wealth management as well as barriers, which are predominantly of a legal and regulatory nature. This is complemented by a discussion of global developments which impact cross-border wealth management. These include recent developments in tax harmonization and tax transparency and a number of economic and political risks. The presentation includes examples from Liechtenstein, Switzerland, Austria, and Germany.

1 Introduction

This article examines to what extent borders impact on wealth management. For this purpose, drawing on examples from Liechtenstein, Switzerland, Austria, and Germany, we illustrate the benefits and costs associated with cross-border wealth management, outline global developments in cross-border wealth management, and identify questions for future research from an economic, legal, and tax perspective.

The article is structured as follows. In Sect. 2, we examine the **drivers of cross-border wealth management and cross-border structures**. All in all, sound economic, legal, and tax drivers provide the background for cross-border wealth

M. Angerer (✉) · M. Hanke · T. Kirn · M. Wenz · M. Amann
University of Liechtenstein, Vaduz, Liechtenstein
e-mail: martin.angerer@uni.li; michael.hanke@uni.li; tanja.kirn@uni.li; martin.wenz@uni.li

C. Preiner
Gasser Partner Rechtsanwälte, Vaduz, Liechtenstein
e-mail: christina.preiner@gasserpartner.com

D. Zetzsche
University of Luxembourg, Vaduz, Liechtenstein
e-mail: dirk.zetzsche@uni.lu

P. Droege et al. (eds.), *Cross-Border Life and Work*, Contributions to Management Science, https://doi.org/10.1007/978-3-031-34362-9_4

management. While tax and regulatory arbitrage opportunities may provide one factor for structuring wealth cross-border, we argue that cross-border wealth management is imperative even in the absence of regulatory arbitrage, given that the most important drivers of cross-border wealth management include (a) given circumstances due to individual mobility, (b) cross-border asset diversification, (c) taking advantage of local expertise, (d) and a centralized management approach.

Section 3 examines **barriers for cross-border wealth management**. Barriers are predominantly of a legal nature. Licensing schemes—in the absence of cross-border passports—are generally speaking limited to national territory, and so is the private law effect of national laws. Hence, cross-border structures create additional public and international private law complexity. From a tax perspective, we analyze the impact of tightening of regulations: the European equivalence requirement as laid down in the AIFMD, MiFID II, and other European regulations for cross-border wealth management requires tax cooperation and tax transparency. In addition, FATCA and CRS enhance tax transparency in cross-border business. We observe certain costs associated with the repatriation and regularization of assets, as well as costs that arise from the transfer to nonbankable assets. High complexity with regard to legal and tax considerations leads to additional costs resulting from additional legal and tax advice from an economic point of view.

Section 4 takes the bird's-eye view and outlines **global developments that impact on cross-border wealth management**. From an economic perspective, currency risks are the main challenge of cross-border wealth management. More precisely, economic and political risks, which are components of currency risks, are the driving impact factors. From a legal perspective, concerns regarding the degree of legal certainty, as well as the degree of discretion to tailor structures according to the investors' needs in light of the ongoing global and regional harmonization, provide challenges. From a tax perspective, the main concerns for cross-border wealth management include the degree of tax harmonization, the increasing cooperation and automatic exchange of information among the most important jurisdictions, as well as the extent to which tax optimization is limited; the latter regards the disregard of double-zero taxation and increasing pressures against purely tax optimized structures without substance and regional wealth generation.

2 Drivers of Cross-Border Wealth Management from the Investors' Perspective

2.1 Mobility

Financial services are highly international. This is not only because financial services are temporarily and locally flexible, but also because know-how, infrastructure, and distribution markets are not necessarily located in the same jurisdiction. The high mobility of financial services has even intensified through innovation and technical development. Harmonization and liberalization of laws foster cross-border activities and create global markets.

In today's economies, also the international mobility of individuals and families is high. Business activities are global, and individuals move between various jurisdictions for personal or professional reasons. With every relocation, the individual leaves behind existing property relations or pension entitlements and establishes new connections.

One of the most important reasons for the existence of cross-border wealth management is the fact that for many investors (mostly, but not limited to, high-net-worth individuals), their assets are located across different countries from the outset. Some assets, such as real estate, are linked to a specific jurisdiction. Viewed in this way, cross-border management of these assets is a naturally arising requirement rather than a conscious choice.

For other financial assets, it would in theory be possible to move them all to one jurisdiction and hence to avoid cross-border management. However, cross-border management can also be advantageous from an economic point of view. Diversification is one major driver, but locational advantages also play an important role, with political stability and local expertise both being examples of this. Both diversification and locational advantages lead to geographical dispersion of assets.

For the resulting complexity of decisions that bring a large number of potential side effects, centralized management is required for a better coordination of the multiple specialists involved and is essential for a holistic wealth management approach, as opposed to a fragmented management of various parts of the portfolio. These aspects require a broad international perspective to cross-border wealth management and wealth structures catered to the needs of the investors and their actual circumstances. In designing those structures, one must take a comprehensive view in which economic, legal, and tax considerations are linked with each other.

2.2 *Diversification*

Diversification is one of the oldest and simplest risk management methods, and its formalization within the context of portfolio theory goes back to Markowitz (1952, 1970). Its purpose is to avoid concentration risks, that is, to reduce potential losses that might result from putting all one's eggs into one basket. Diversification applies to different risk dimensions, that is, asset classes, maturity structures, counterparties, and—the most important dimension when it comes to cross-border management—geographical regions.

At the core of the principle of diversification, we have the fundamental insight that whereas higher (expected) returns can only be achieved by taking more risk (if starting from an efficient, i.e., already well-diversified portfolio), the converse is not necessarily true: higher risk only increases expected returns if the risk is rewarded in the market. As a rule, investors cannot expect a premium for taking risks that can easily be avoided and which are therefore not priced. For many asset classes, concentration risk is one of those risks that are quite easy to avoid. Using the example of geographical diversification, the concentration of an investor's assets in one particular country or region increases risk but leads to lower expected returns compared to a portfolio with a wider geographical diversification. The benefits of international diversification are well-documented in the literature. [1] In the light of these results, overweighting of geographically closely located assets appears to be a harmful behavioral bias, which is widespread and which is known as the "home bias" in the behavioral financial economics literature. [2]

How easy it is to avoid concentration risk varies for different asset classes. For stocks in publicly traded companies, broad geographical diversification is very easy to achieve. For other asset classes, such as stakes in non-traded companies or real estate, the costs and risks involved may be substantial and often increase with the geographical distance between the assets and the investor.

2.3 *Locational Advantages*

When organizing wealth management structures, there is typically more than one way to do so. Similar results can be achieved via a number of different jurisdictions. [3] Due to the fact that financial services move easily across borders, one is able to obtain the best results by leveraging various jurisdictions. This refers to expertise, regulatory environment, and legal infrastructure as well as to economic and tax considerations.

2.3.1 Economics

Depending on the type of assets, the spectrum of locational advantages may be quite broad. Examples include low wage costs, availability of specialist know-how, political as well as economic stability, and local expertise. In economic terms, they all boil down essentially to the costs and risks associated with having assets in a particular location. An assessment of these always has to take into account both the present and the future: higher costs in the present may be acceptable in stable

[1] See, e.g., French and Poterba French, K. R., & Poterba, J. M. (1991). Investor diversification and international equity markets. *American Economic Review*, 81(2), 222–226. or Odier and Solnik Odier, P., & Solnik, B. (1993). Lessons for international asset allocation. *Financial Analysts Journal*, 49(2), 63–77.

[2] See French and Poterba French, K. R., & Poterba, J. M. (1991). Investor diversification and international equity markets. *American Economic Review*, 81(2), 222–226. or Tesar and Werner Tesar, L. L., & Werner, I. M. (1995). Home bias and high turnover. *Journal of international money and finance*, 14(4), 467–492.

[3] The same "economic substance" may be given different "legal forms"; see Fleischer, V. (2010). Regulatory arbitrage. *Texas Law Review*, 89(2), 227–290.

countries, given that relocation of assets in case of political turmoil may be either impossible or associated with very high costs. Stability in this regard includes also the legal and tax systems: the more frequently changes occur there, the higher the locational advantages in other fields must be in a particular geographical region to outweigh the economic costs of repeatedly having to revise structures with an eye on legal security and tax optimality.

2.3.2 Legal

Optimizing Legal Designs

Every jurisdiction offers structures that can be used for wealth management purposes. However, there are jurisdictions that traditionally have a stronger market for wealth management. Those jurisdictions offer specific legal instruments for wealth management purposes and are therefore ideal to solve complex structuring challenges.

In the context of a family business, for example, the fragmentation of control surrounding the family business over generations can present an issue. In this context, foundation and trust structures may serve those structuring needs and allow the separation of assets and control. If the home jurisdiction of the family business does not offer similar tools, the family may profit from using foreign wealth management structures to serve their structuring needs. However, the question lies in whether the home country recognizes the foreign entity. In Switzerland, the use of family foundations is restricted to mitigate the costs of raising, endowing, or supporting family members and therefore of limited use for wealth management purposes (Jacob and Studen 2016, p. 707). [4]

The usage of regulated structures, such as investment funds, for private wealth management purposes strongly depends on the product regulation in the respective jurisdiction. If the investment strategy for private investor funds is determined in detail by the regulator, the respective jurisdiction may not be eligible for the purpose of private wealth management. [5]

---

[4] According to Art. 154 in conjunction with Art. 17 of the Swiss IPRG, is the incorporation theory applicable to foreign structures, if that structure is not deemed to be manifestly contrary to the Swiss public policy? This is according to BGE 135 III 614 not the case for Liechtenstein foundations.

[5] See, for example, the German KAGB, e.g., §§ 218, 221, 231 KAGB, and for closed-ended AIF § 261 et seq KAGB versus Art. 16 in conjunction with Art. 91 Li-AIFMG in conjunction with Art. 154 et seq. Li-AIFMV.

Access to Markets, Know-How, and Regulation

The specific appeal of a certain economic era, jurisdiction, or financial center spurs cross-border activity. We have identified three main reasons of attraction: access to know-how, access to markets, and access to favorable regulation.

Access to know-how is the most important soft factor in the competition between jurisdictions and the one factor that is most difficult to establish. Financial services consist to a large extent of intellectual property. Specific financial services are best obtained in areas where there is a yearlong experience in the field and the relevant skills are developed. This is one of the reasons why financial centers play an important role in cross-border wealth management. They accumulate intellectual property and legal infrastructure necessary to attract customers also from other areas of the world (Zetzsche 2016).

Another significant factor is market access. To be profitable, some products must be sold to a relatively high number of investors. Therefore, in order to facilitate the sales of investment products, marketing in other jurisdictions and big distribution markets is necessary. [6] In order to obtain financial services, it is not necessary to move physically, because financial services may be obtained via the Internet or from other means far away. However, in order to have access to investors in certain jurisdictions, it is advisable to be located under the respective law or in a jurisdiction with equivalent regulatory standards. Sometimes the market access for foreign products is restricted. In order to have access to the European market, for example, intermediaries and products must be located in third countries that cooperate with the EU in financial supervision or exchange of information. [7]

Restructuring, relocation, and cross-border activity are also ways to achieve access to favorable regulation. Depending on the perspective, favorable regulation might mean high reputation (and high cost), low cost (and low reputation), or a combination of both. One may be able to significantly reduce regulatory costs by opting for one or the other jurisdiction. Regulatory costs may stem from onerous regulatory standards with respect to organization or regulatory capital or restrictive rules on remuneration. A favorable regulatory environment, however, may also mean having an experienced and fast supervisory architecture. Furthermore, the reputation of a jurisdiction or a specific product-brand may be the decisive factor of going cross-border. Some jurisdictions or brands suggest a high level of investor protection or a specific regulatory standard that investors are looking for in their

[6] For the distinction distribution markets versus production states, see Zetzsche Zetzsche, D. (2016). Competitiveness of financial centers in light of financial and tax law equivalence requirements. In E. Buckley, E. Avgouleas, & D. W. Arner (Eds.), *Reconceptualising Global Finance and its Regulation* (pp. 390–418). Cambridge: Cambridge University Press, Zetzsche, D. (2014. "Drittstaaten" im Europäischen Bank-und Finanzmarktrecht. In B. G., & B. Breig (Eds.), *Finanzmarktregulierung zwischen Innovation und Kontinuität* (pp. 48–140). Tübingen: Mohr Siebeck.

[7] Art. 35 para 2 AIFMD.

due-diligence process (European Commission 2012, p. 53); the usage of the UCITS or ELTIF brand is restricted to EU products only. [8]

2.3.3 Taxation

Individual income tax planning and wealth transfer tax planning are important aspects of cross-border wealth management. The tax efficiency of wealth management structures can be increased, if locational advantages of different tax domiciles are beneficially combined. In doing so, cross-border wealth planning includes the choice of structure and jurisdiction.

The choice of structure depends on numerous criteria, like the capabilities to consolidate assets under one structure, the possibility of reserving investment power and control over investments, the possibility of succession planning, and the suitability for tax planning. As the legal concept of structure instruments depends on national law, the choice of the structure is often intertwined with choice of location. Commonly used wealth planning instruments are private foundations and private trusts. Whereas the legal concept of the private foundation derives from civil law, a private trust derives from common law. Liechtenstein is the only continental European country which has codified the foundation as well as the common-law trust. Due to increasing internationalization, however, private law legal concepts are gaining acceptance in common-law jurisdictions and vice versa. Hence, the structural and locational choice does not limit cross-border capital mobility.

Due to the increasing internationalization and recognition of legal structures, the choice of jurisdiction from the perspective of tax efficiency depends on the possibilities of international tax arbitrage and the availability of double-taxation agreements to prevent double taxation.

2.4 Centralized Management: Holistic Wealth Management Approach

With assets in different countries for the reasons discussed above, a centralized management of these dispersed assets is essential to implement a holistic wealth management approach, as opposed to fragmented management of parts of the portfolio (Fazzi 2005). From a tax and legal point of view, the advantages of such a centralized management are obvious. Tax efficiency, for instance, would be next to impossible to achieve in a decentralized structure, and issues like wealth fragmentation or asset protection also lead quite naturally to centralized management.

However, centralized management is also essential from an economic point of view, simply because the aggregate of optimal solutions in each of the parts of a

[8] Art. 1 para 1 UCITSD; Art. 3 para 2 ELTIFR.

portfolio does not, in general, lead to an overall optimum for the entire portfolio. Unfortunately, many investors suffer from a well-documented psychological bias in this regard, which is known as "mental accounting" (Thaler 1985). It causes investors to mentally subdivide their wealth into different (fictitious) accounts, each of which is then managed and evaluated more or less separately. Assets that are located in different geographical regions or jurisdictions are particularly prone to such mental accounting. This means that mental accounting plays an important (and detrimental) role in cross-border wealth management, and advisors as well as investors should be aware of it.

One example for such a centralized management, which makes sense only for high levels of wealth, is family offices. Aside from other functions they usually perform for investors, holistic optimization of the asset allocation (taking all assets into account) is one of their most important tasks. In this optimization, the constraints determined by the investors' personal situation and preferences play an important role. This renders this task as highly complex and individualized and prevents it from being standardized. Family offices play an important role in the investment management and oversight: whereas, e.g., day-to-day management of companies that are part of the assets is best delegated to local specialists, detecting new and potentially interesting investments as well as regular revisions of the existing portfolio would be done by the family office (on top of tax-efficiency issues like size and timing of distributions).

For the location of the family office, political stability and the local availability of the required expertise are important factors. The level of local labor costs typically plays a less important role (if at all), in particular for higher wealth levels: in light of the risks involved to the estate and given the small relative costs of the central management compared to total wealth, it should not come as a surprise that many family offices are located in countries with high wage levels.

2.5 *Taxation*

In a closed economic environment, corporate taxation is relatively straightforward, but it becomes more complex when operations are spread across different countries (cross-border perspective). Basically, corporations are required to pay taxes on their total income, no matter where they originate from. However, through the circumstance of double taxation, rising in the early days of globalization, three pillars of international taxation have been stated in Coates (1924).

These consist first of source-based taxation, second of the "arm's length" principle, and third of more than 3000 bilateral tax agreements. All three principles provide their own opportunities for cross-border tax optimization. A famous example, demonstrating the narrow boundary between the exploitation and abuse of available legislation, is demonstrated by a court decision in 1997 by the Bundesfinanzhof (Germany). The court overruled a structure consisting of a Dutch foundation holding the total shares of two Dutch stock corporations, which formed a civil-law partnership and require real estate in Germany. The purchase was financed by a loan granted by the foundation. The cost of interest further exceeded the rental income and therefore did not provide any income tax base. Finally, the reason for the overruling according to §42 AO was that the civil-law partnership had no additional taxable activities. Aggressive tax planning in the form of structures like these has been one of the key drivers behind latest efforts of the international community (G7/G20/OECD) to prevent such actions. One of the highly debated projects is the so-called OECD Base Erosion and Profit Shifting (BEPS) project; another is the so-called EU Anti-Tax Avoidance Package (ATAP).

In the following chapters, we will therefore evaluate the existing benefits of the three-pillar system to investors with cross-border ambitions and illustrate possible inadvertent long-term consequences of BEPS actions to economic growth.

2.5.1 Tailoring Taxation to Investor Base

Example 1: Widely Spread Mutual Funds

Changes in demographics, the abolishment of capital controls, as well as technology and financial instrument innovations have led to soaring inflows to collective investment vehicles, such as mutual funds, over the last two decades. Through their significant economic impact, academics have dedicated a lot of research to the dependencies between mutual fund investment strategies and tax rules. Sialm et al. (2015), for example, explore the impact of tax efficient investment strategies on mutual fund returns. They calculated that, only through the different tax rates between short- and long-term capital gains, the return of a $10,000 initial investment in 1990 is reduced from $48,818 to $37,850 in 2012. However, short- and long-term capital gains are not the only factor when it comes to investment income taxation. Another factor is the classification of the investor himself. In the USA, for example, close to 50% of mutual fund investments are ascribable to tax-qualified investors, such as pension funds. This requires mutual fund managers to tailor the tax efficiency of their investments to their investor base. The higher the proportion of tax-qualified investors, the higher the distribution of gains. Although this pattern can be mostly observed on a national level, Christoffersen et al. (2005) point out hurdles in cross-border application. Cross-border dividends often incur foreign withholding tax (WHT) which is, depending on the double-taxation agreement between the corresponding countries, not reclaimable. The majority of the literature distinguishes in the investment fund set up between the two- and three-country case. While in the two country case the foreign source corporation is located in the same country as the collective investment scheme (CIS), the CIS is placed in a third country in the course of the three-country case. The source country's WHT rate, the creditability of the withholding tax, non-creditable income tax on the CIS, and the conversion from dividends into gains are the main considerations (OECD 1999, p. 58).

Lissi and Utzinger (2016) show by the example of Switzerland that there are obstacles and hurdles for cross-border investors with respect to the WHT. First, they note that for "open-end" foreign CIS, characterized by taxation at investor level, Switzerland's double-taxation treaties are in general not eligible to reclaim WHT. However, there are a few exceptions which highlight the efforts taken to enhance cross-border economic activity. Bilateral agreements exist, for example, with "Australia, Austria, Canada, Denmark, Germany, France, Norway, Spain, Sweden, the Netherlands and the UK" (Lissi and Utzinger 2016), enabling "open-end" CIS there to reclaim the WHT. In addition, they identify the high WHT as a competitive disadvantage for the Swiss fund market in general. To maintain the attractiveness of Switzerland for the fund industry, non-Swiss residents are exempted from the WHT if 80% or more of the CIS income is generated from abroad, displaying the potential benefits of the three-country case.

Alternatively, the foreign withholding tax can also be offset at the third country level by applying a bilateral tax agreement. However, nontaxable investors, such as mutual funds, can usually not benefit from the offset of the foreign WHT. Therefore, mutual funds and other nontaxable accounts are reluctant to cross-border dividends and prefer long-term capital gains instead. Christoffersen et al. (2005) offer a practical perspective by taking lending agreements into account to avoid the WHT in the first place. However, their data show that through the lending of the securities back to a source state resident borrower for the dividend record-dates, only a fraction of the not creditable WHT can be converted into cash, leaving cross-border dividends a net tax for nontaxable accounts.

The OECD initiated rulebook on base erosion and profit shifting as currently proposed would have a profound impact on cross-border investment funds, such as mutual funds. Action 6 of BEPS regarding tax treaty abuse even relates directly to collective investment vehicles (CIVs) such as mutual funds. Subparagraph 2f is meant to be drafted dependent on the treatment and use of CIVs in the corresponding contracting state. Even though the action plan maintains the possibility for third state residents to enjoy the treaty benefits, through respective formulation of subparagraph 2f, the CIV must be held by equivalent beneficiaries. This regulation prevents the application of CIVs for certain user groups such as family offices and corporates.

Example 2: Family Office

Through the increasing mobility of family members and the worldwide allocation of assets, family offices (FOs) are particularly affected by cross-border regulations. Since especially Switzerland is an attractive location for FOs, Switzerland will be used as an example within this paper, due to its central position within Europe and its cross-border integration (Bader et al. 2015).

A FO is not a separate legal form; however, they are often organized as a limited (Ltd.) or public limited company (PLC) to achieve simple ownership rulings (Bader et al. 2015). The ownership function can be either perceived by any natural person, trust, or foundation which will result in different tax implications. From the point of view of taxation, besides the tax burden on the entity level (corporate income tax and capital tax), FO clients focus on capital gain taxes.

In Switzerland, the capital gain tax amounts to 35% and is refundable for Swiss citizens who properly declare their dividend income in their income tax form. Generally speaking, this holds true for foreign beneficiaries. However, every bilateral double-taxation treaty includes non-recoverable WHT raising similar issues for FOs as for mutual fund clients. While capital gain taxes can ultimately only be reduced, the capital accumulation can be considerable facilitated by the formation of a FO. Bader et al. (2015) postulate that FO holdings exceeding 25% for more than 2 years are exempted from tax duties on the FO level. As abovementioned, every FO beneficiary has his own specific requirements for reaching maximal tax efficiency. To find a common denominator for all, independent from their country of residence or categorization, flow-through entities—such as income trusts—can improve after-tax returns noticeable.

If the holding function is perceived by a foundation, the specific arrangement of the foundation is decisive for the tax status. In detail, the transparent or nontransparent taxable character depends on the degree of economic connectivity of the beneficiaries. In case of transparency, the current income is attributed directly to the beneficiary and taxed in his residency country. In case of nontransparent foundations, the income is attributed to the foundation, and it is subject to the corporate income tax (Marschner 2015, pp. 196–197).

2.5.2 Optimizing Taxation on the Entity Level

Corporate Income Tax

A significant portion of cross-border investments is done by corporations directly. Hereby, the form of investment is the main consideration for foreign corporations besides economic reasonability and the category of resulting income (Höhn and Höring 2010, p. 77). The investment form can either be direct business (e.g., export) or direct investment (e.g., permanent establishment, subsidiary). If a foreign entity opts for direct business, the total income generated thereby is taxed in the country of sale, in case of no existing double-taxation agreement. The limited tax liability can, for example, be triggered by the provision of services and the allocation of intellectual property rights and other items, as far as they are not provided by a local permanent establishment (p. 85). The foreign direct investment, often perceived by a permanent establishment (PE), is compared to the foreign subsidiary with no independent legal entity. This characteristic offers besides its advantages such as fast and low-cost execution also disadvantages by allowing fewer possibilities for contractual arrangements between the parent company and the PE (p. 87). However, due to the inconsistent PE definitions at national level, the PE is a popular instrument for global tax planning. However, the most popular outbound-investment instrument is the foreign subsidiary. This follows from the limited liability and the independent legal entity character of the subsidiary. A further advantage of this particular company structure is the opacity. Companies are not taxed on their profits until they are distributed. Another important factor for the popularity of the foreign subsidiary is the "parent companies/subsidiaries" directive adopted by the European Council. This directive exempts foreign subsidiaries of the withholding tax if the participation threshold of 10% is exceeded by the parent company within the European Union (EU) (European Commission 2016). For the future, the European Commission is planning further initiatives such as the Common Consolidated Corporate Tax Base (CCCTB), with the primary goal of reducing the compliance costs for corporations. Especially among SMEs, the compliance costs are estimated at 30% of the tax liability (Jacob and Studen 2016, p. 229). Further goals are the prevention of double taxation, cross-border loss compensation, and enabling tax-neutral cross-border restructuring. All these proposals are meant to enhance cross-border investment conditions; however, they noticeably restrict tax competition.

Tax on Transactions

The main taxes on corporate transactions are the so-called stamp duty on certain financial services, real estate transfer taxes, and value added tax (VAT). While the first two focus on corporate transactions, the VAT is payable on the supply of goods or services by businesses that are taxpayers for VAT purposes. Because of the Customs Union Agreement of March 29, 1923, all transaction taxes are equally applicable in Switzerland and Liechtenstein, which facilitates cross-border transactions for Liechtenstein based investors.

The Swiss "stamp duty" comprises the securities transfer stamp tax and the securities issuance stamp tax (as defined in the Swiss Federal Stamp Duty Act). The securities transfer stamp tax is payable on the transfer of taxable securities, such as shares, bonds, and investments in collective investment schemes, by the securities dealer. Securities dealers are banks and Swiss companies that hold securities with a tax book value of more than CHF 10 million, according to their balance sheet. The tax rate is 0.15% for Swiss securities and 0.3% if foreign securities are transferred. The securities transfer stamp tax is payable by the securities dealer, but it is usually based on contractual obligations borne by the counterparties. The securities transfer stamp tax on the sale of shares can be avoided if the shares are transferred in a tax-neutral restructuring or if the proceeds from the sale of a participation of at least 10% are used to acquire an interest in another company that is to be reinvested in order to be eligible for a rollover relief. However, in the cross-border context, it is only applicable if a domestic securities dealer is involved as a party or as an intermediary to the transaction. The residence of the seller or buyer of shares is not of relevance.

Securities issuance stamp tax is triggered when a shareholder contribution to a Swiss resident company's equity exceeds CHF 1 million, regardless of whether the contributions occur in cash or in kind. In cases where the Swiss stamp duty is not applicable due to differing private law regulations, a Liechtenstein-specific issuance stamp tax is levied. The issuance stamp tax ranges from 1% for the first CHF 5 million to 0.5% for contributions of over CHF 5 million and 0.3% for contributions of over CHF 10 million. The exemption threshold of CHF 1 million applies. Reorganizations such as spin-offs of corporate assets, mergers, or relocations from abroad are typically excluded. Foreign companies are not subject to securities issuance stamp tax if they are not domiciled in Switzerland/Liechtenstein or are effectively managed and controlled from there.

VAT applies to the sale of goods and services in Liechtenstein and to the import of goods and services to Liechtenstein. Liechtenstein is considered part of Switzerland for VAT purposes, based on the 1923 Customs Union Agreement. The standard VAT rate is 8%. Certain goods and services are subject to a reduced rate of 2.5%, and others (e.g., financial services, real estate transactions, transaction of securities including shares) are exempted. Exports of goods and services are, in principle, zero-rated. Enterprises whose annual turnover exceeds CHF 100,000 must register for VAT purposes. With regard to transfers at the entity level, VAT may become due if any rights, in particular IP rights, are sold (treated as a provision of services) or if assets are transferred (taxable delivery of goods). The transfer of a business as a going concern is subject to VAT, but instead of paying the tax, the parties must apply a notification procedure. If a cross-border activity is carried out by a Swiss/FL PE of a foreign corporation, it may be subject to VAT. Additionally, a foreign company that supplies goods and services within the Swiss-Liechtenstein customs union may also become liable to VAT.

2.5.3 Optimizing Taxation on the Investor Level

Tax planning at the investor level entails determining the best "place" to own a particular investment. Investments of high-net-worth individuals are rarely kept in just one account or entity. Instead, they are usually held in various buckets set up to implement the investor's financial and wealth transfer planning over time. One aim of this strategic asset allocation is to achieve tax efficient portfolio. Another aspect of tax optimization concerns estate planning, as many investors will not consume all of their wealth in their lifetimes and will leave an estate to others.

Tax Management

A tax efficient portfolio requires that the investor determines how the accounts are structured under the law which is applicable in the respective entities. Generally speaking, accounts can be taxable, tax deferred, or tax exempt. For taxable accounts, like individual and joint investment accounts, bank accounts, and money market mutual funds, investors must pay taxes on their investment income in the year it was received. However, tax-deferred accounts shelter investments from taxes as long as they remain in the account. Examples of tax-deferred accounts are retirement accounts, the US 401(k) plan, IRA, or Roth IRA. For tax-exempt accounts, investors do not need to pay taxes even at withdrawal.

In addition, investors must also be aware of the different tax implications of current income and capital gains. Whereas current income is generally taxable at the investor's bracket rate, capital gains are distinguished by being either short term (usually realized by assets held less than 1 year) or long term (assets usually held more than 1 year). While short-term capital gains are generally taxed at the investor's marginal tax bracket, long-term rates are taxed at a preferential rate. In order to reduce the tax burden, investors should therefore try to generate capital gains which will be taxed at the preferential longer-term rate.

Furthermore, the tax benefits of harvesting capital losses must be taken into account (Arnott et al. 2001). Tax-loss harvesting is a strategy of selling an investment that has an unrealized loss, thus realizing the loss, and crediting it against realized capital gains generated by the portfolio. To maintain the expected risk and return level of the portfolio, the asset sold is then replaced with a very similar asset. In doing so, tax-loss harvesting is a tool to limit the recognition of short-term capital gains, in order to increase after-tax returns of the portfolio (Berkin and Ye 2003; Chincarini and Kim 2001; Horvitz and Wilcox 2003; Stein and Narasimhan 1999).

Estate Planning

Intergenerational estate planning requires a profound understanding of regulatory and legal structures, such as foundations and trusts, as well as income and estate taxes. Although managing exposure to estate tax is a task in its own right, it overlaps considerably with investment management.

The first step of integrating estate planning and investment decisions is to determine the capital required to secure an investor's standard of living (so-called core capital). Based on this, the wealth manager can then develop strategies to transfer available capital in excess of this amount to others (heirs, charitable endeavors) without jeopardizing consumption goals. Although the legal recognition and tax treatment of estate vary between jurisdictions, foundations, trusts, life insurance, companies, and family limited partnerships (FLPs) are common estate planning structures (Jennings et al. 2011).

From a tax perspective, life insurance policies can be attractive from several points of view. First, the death benefit proceeds paid to life insurance beneficiaries are tax exempt in many countries. Second, insurance premiums paid by the policyholder are not part of the policyholder's taxable estate at the time of death and thus not subject to an estate tax. Third, life insurance payments can be used by the heirs to pay inheritance tax triggered by the wealth owner's death (Jennings et al. 2011). Hence, life insurance policies could be used as a liquidity management tool that generates liquidity to pay estate taxes.

3 Costs of Cross-Border Wealth Management

The cost *categories* of cross-border wealth management are in principle identical to those of wealth management without the cross-border dimension, but the levels of the various categories are different if assets are managed across borders. The increased complexity brought about by the geographical dispersion of assets requires specialists in the areas of asset allocation and advisory services. Drafting contracts involving several jurisdictions is clearly more demanding compared to the purely domestic case, and the same holds for tax and regulatory issues. The required expertise can usually be found only in selected regions of the world, which are typically regions with comparatively high salaries. For complex structures, this means that the wealth threshold beyond which the cost-benefit analysis becomes favorable can be quite high. Depending on the range of services offered and the type of assets involved, the wealth levels required for family offices are reported to be between 100 and 700 million USD. As a result, in recent years, a trend has emerged toward pooling of services, e.g., in the form of multifamily offices, which offer their services to several families as opposed to single-family offices (Family Office Council 2015). Provided that the families involved share certain core values, this seems to be an efficient organizational structure to better utilize the resources invested into the centralized management.

3.1 Legal Complexity

Differences in legal systems and the adaption to them are one of the core drivers of costs of cross-border wealth management. This refers to initial costs when setting up a structure as well as ongoing monitoring of compliance. These are costs for consultancy and legal advice, for staff training, and for administration of different IT systems. Furthermore, one has to account for the potential costs linked to legal risks that stem from the misconception of foreign rules (those will be discussed later).

In the financial services sector, not only does the private law dimension present a challenge to market participants, but also financial regulation in the relevant jurisdiction. While some intermediaries and products have always been confronted with these two dimensions of legal complexity, the financial crisis led to the extension of regulation on a variety of products that were once only subject to private law (so-called proliferation of financial law) (Arner et al. 2016). Each additional requirement and approval procedure of course raises the cost of cross-border wealth management.

3.1.1 Public Law Dimension

The public law dimension deals with the access to a foreign jurisdiction. It erects barriers for market access of two kinds: first, preventive bans from the home market for unauthorized products and intermediaries and, second, prohibitive costs associated with strongly varying regulatory requirements.

Public law traditionally serves the purpose to protect investors and the market from poorly managed or fraudulent market participants. The scope of protection and the mandate of the respective competent authority are in principle confined to the borders of the respective state. [9] In order to mitigate the risks that are associated with potentially poor regulated foreign financial intermediaries, states conduct an autonomous licensing or authorization process for foreign products and intermediaries. Business activity is prohibited subject to prior approval by the competent authorities. Entering an authorization process is of course subject to a charge in every jurisdiction. Those multiple licensing and authorization procedures are therefore time-consuming and costly.

Regulatory requirements in the various jurisdictions can differ significantly. Some activities may be subject to supervision within one jurisdiction while being unregulated in another. For example, individual portfolio management has been regulated within the EEA since 1993 [10] and has remained subject to self-regulation in Switzerland up to the present day. [11] Also, divergent regulation can be nothing less than burdensome. Sometimes intermediaries will even face conflicting requirements in two different jurisdictions. The expenses to adapt to every target country may render the cross-border activity ineffective.

The first barrier, being the additional licensing and authorization processes, is overcome by multilateral agreements and mutual recognition of supervision between the respective jurisdictions. The different regulatory requirements in various jurisdictions as a second barrier are vanquished by the harmonization of financial regulation. Harmonization happens in a mutual process by two or more jurisdictions or via voluntary alignment by one jurisdiction to the regulation of another. Of course, harmonization of law and market access are mostly communicating pipes. Both will be discussed later in more detail.

[9] See for Liechtenstein Art. 4 FMAG; for Switzerland Art. 5 FINMAG; for Austria § 1 FMABG; for Germany § 4 FinDAG.

[10] Council Directive 93/22/EEC of May 10, 1993, on investment services in the securities field.

[11] See however the legislative process concerning the Federal Financial Services Act (FinSA) and Financial Institutions Act (FinIA).

3.1.2 Private Law Dimension

Private laws of member states have, albeit influenced by each other, grown historically. Distinct legal traditions and legal culture render private law less open for harmonization. [12] Thus, the private law in the European Union is, apart from common historic foundations, highly fragmented. This has an impact on cross-border wealth management that should not be underestimated. Gaps, overlaps, and contradictions in the interplay between jurisdictions are the consequence. As every financial service and financial product is rooted in private law, even a full harmonization of financial services law cannot compensate the risk and costs associated with this fragmentation.

There are, however, three major sources of convergence in the field of private law. First, the free choice of law is possible under many jurisdictions and spurs legal competition and convergence (Eidenmüller 2011; Vogenauer 2013). Second, the initiatives for common standards in private law, such as the "Draft Common Frame of Reference" (DCFR) or the Proposal for a Common European Sales Law (CESL) by the European Commission, provide an alternative to the harmonization of national laws. Third, the judgments of the ECJ in the field of company law have led to an opening toward full cross-border mobility and recognition of foreign companies (Borg Barthet 2010).

Private International Law Dimension: Which Private Law Applies?

When financial services cross borders, the question as to which law applies may already be highly complex. For example, the traditional lex rei sitae approach in private international law for cross-border securities transactions is problematic because securities nowadays are nothing similar to movable tangible property (Kozey 2015; Rogers 2006; Thévenoz 2013). It is however vital for the correct creation and evaluation of a legal position.

Free choice of law can be a tool to reduce legal uncertainty as to which law would be applicable (Eidenmüller 2011, p. 711). Within the European Union, the freedom of choice is granted, albeit in some areas restricted with respect to consumer protection considerations, in the field of contract law as well as in the field of company and tax law (Vogenauer 2013).

[12] A detailed analysis of opponents and supporters of a European corporate law and its recent developments provides Hopt Hopt, K. J. (2015). Corporate governance in Europe: A critical review of the European Commission's initiatives on corporate law and corporate governance. *New York University Journal of Law & Business*, 12(1), 139–213.

Recognition of Foreign Entities?

A legal person is, other than a natural person, basically a construct of a specific legal system. Consequently, the transposition of a legal person from one jurisdiction to another can be difficult. Rules regarding liability, governance, the board, or the minimum capital differ (Rammeloo 2003, p. 170). When we transpose a legal person cross-border, we are confronted with the question of whether the rules of the home jurisdiction (incorporation) or the rules of the host jurisdiction (seat) apply. Tied to this question is the acknowledgement of the structure as legal person and therefore, for example, its capacity to enforce contractual rights as well as the acknowledgment of certain features such as a separation of assets, as regulated under the governing law in the state of incorporation (Borg Barthet 2010, p. 594; Butterstein 2015, p. 3; Rammeloo 2003, p. 170). We solve these questions through the conflict of law rules. With the incorporation theory and the real seat doctrine, there are two basic approaches (Rammeloo 2003, p. 172). Under the incorporation theory, the host country applies the law of the home country to the structure, whereas under the seat theory, the structure would be reinterpreted under the host countries' laws.

Within the European Union, companies must be able to use the treaty freedoms to go cross-border. Following a number of ECJ judgments, the incorporation theory has prevailed. Beginning with Centros in 1999, [13] they have led to an opening toward full cross-border mobility. Companies can migrate cross borders within the European Union and must be recognized, if they are incorporated within a member state (Borg Barthet 2010, p. 594). Also, under Art. 154 of the Swiss IPRG, the incorporation theory applies. This is unless the structure is deemed to be manifestly contrary to the Swiss public policy (Art. 17 of the Swiss IPRG).

Differences in private law can, however, still be impediments to cross-border activity, for example, if the foreign entities used are not recognized or misunderstood in the home country of the relevant individuals. For certain vehicles frequently used for the structuring of private wealth, such as foundations or trusts, legal certainty is not yet given (Butterstein 2015, p. 3). Often lawyers and judges of civil-law jurisdictions are unfamiliar with the concept of a trust and the delineation between legal and equitable ownership. This may lead to wrongful reinterpretations of the nature of a trust and the legal position of a trustee (Bösch 2015, p. 150). Not only misinterpretation but also reservations may lead to reinterpretation of a structure. The disregard of separation of the trust property may have severe consequences in case of insolvency of the trustee.

[13] ECJ, 09.03.1999 - C-212/97-*Centros Ltd.*

3.2 *Taxation*

The costs of cross-border wealth management with regard to taxation arise, at one hand, from tightening of regulations (such as tax transparency, FATCA) and obligations resulting therefrom, such as the need for a regularization of assets, on the other hand, from transactions like the repatriation of assets or the transfers to nonbankable assets.

3.2.1 Tightening of Regulations: MiFID II, Tax Transparency, FATCA, and CRS

The recent financial crisis has led to a thorough overhaul of financial market regulation. The need for a global regulatory framework for international financial markets is based on numerous and interdependent factors. First is the economic globalization that goes along with an increasing number of financial institutions with global reach and systemic importance. Second is the increasing complexity, exemplified by the rapid growth of structured products and derivatives as well as the growing role played by less-regulated entities such as the structured investment vehicles (International Monetary Fund 2008). Third is the significant cross-national variation in the regulation and supervision of financial sectors, as financial regulators differ in their extent of independence. Without a global framework for the international financial sector, those developments and differences may contribute to systemic risks and facilitate regulatory arbitrage and divergent policy outcomes (Mosely and Singer 2009).

It is argued that the financial crisis was not merely caused by excessive risk-taking and reckless lending but by the fundamental problem of deficient transparency (Friedlander 2015). The crisis showed that financial markets had become dangerously opaque. For example, after the collapse of Lehman Brothers, it was impossible to predict a particulars bank's risk from derivative trading, and hence the interbank market dried up completely. Therefore, in the wake of the financial crisis, the primary global goal was to increase transparency and reduce systemic risk.

However, the increase in transparency has been implemented to varying degrees in the USA and the EU. In the USA, the extension of transparency in Dodd-Frank, among other related legislative frameworks, is limited to derivative markets. In the EU, the Markets in Financial Instruments Directive (MiFID) Review entails the new Directive (MiFID II) and the Markets in Financial Instruments Regulation (MiFIR). As the regulative framework tries to optimize the transaction costs of securities and derivative trading while also taking systemic stability goals into consideration, Europe is going one step further in its transparency requirements. Increasing the transparency is commendable; however, the practicalities of implementing and working with new trading models may increase the complexity and the costs even more than originally anticipated (Achkar 2016). Furthermore, it is argued that the homogeneity induced by a transnational regulatory regime increases the probability of risks being systemic and creating contagion (Morgan and Thorum 2016).

Over the last decade, also the international cooperation in tax matters and tax transparency increased. The first multinational automatic exchange of information (AEoI) program was adopted in 2003 with the EU Savings Directive. This was pursued in 2010 by the US Foreign Account Tax Compliance Act (FATCA). Encouraged by FATCA's momentum, the G20 formally requested the OECD to develop global AEoI standard. In 2014 the OECD released its common reporting standard (CRS) for automatic exchange of information. Nowadays, nearly 100 jurisdictions have implemented the CRS.

The EU adopted the CRS by amending the Directive on Administrative Cooperation. Under the directive, the member states are required to provide financial account information such as investment income (including interest and dividends), account balances, and sales proceeds from financial assets to the tax authorities of other member states. Also, Switzerland introduced AEoI with EU member states and others. The AEoI with these countries entered into force on January 1, 2018, resulting in a data exchange starting in 2019.

Although the CRS is based on FACTA, CRS has a much wider scope than FATCA. CRS has over 80 data elements of which 17 are unique to CRS and only 36% of the elements have the same definition under FATCA (Ernst and Young 2015). Furthermore, the CRS does not include the minimum 50,000 USD threshold meaning that all accounts are subject to potential reporting. Meanwhile, both systems entail due diligence on new and preexisting accounts held by individuals and entities (Christensen and Tirard 2016).

Under both regulations, the information has to be provided by financial institutions to tax authorities, which generates compliance costs. It is argued that the AEoI and greater tax transparency have negatively impacted international wealth management market volume, with some clients repatriating their wealth and returning to domestic wealth managers. However, cross-border wealth management is expected to remain important in the future as high-net-worth individuals (HNWIs) continue to see the benefits of diversifying their wealth globally and to value the expertise of leading wealth managers—although less so than in the past (Lambert 2016).

3.2.2 Repatriation and Regularization of Assets

Traditionally, investors and business owners diversify wealth and investments globally and outside of home jurisdictions. A widely used practice is to set up holding structures including offshore companies and offshore accounts, which often carry the result, if not necessary the intent, of reducing the tax implications. This form of tax planning became in recent years a subject of focus and counteractive measures by governments like the AEoI, FATCA, and CRS that are aiming to fight tax evasion.

Considering the large number of jurisdictions that have committed to CRS and AEoI globally, tax evasion through hiding of assets in a foreign jurisdiction should become impossible and a thing of the past. Taxpayers with undeclared funds held in another country will no longer be able to shelter offshore funds. They need to take urgent note of the fact that they could face significant penalties and even prosecution, as revenue authorities are starting with an AEoI.

In the run-up of the implementation of the AEoI, many governments announced a tax amnesty program which provides a limited time within which tax residents may pay a specific defined tax charge in exchange for forgiveness of outstanding tax liabilities, under which declaration of offshore assets shall be made with or without repatriation. On the one hand, these programs are aimed to deliver cost-efficient improvements in short-term tax revenues, and on the other hand, they are designed to improve longer-term tax compliance. In addition, some programs aim to encourage repatriation of capital invested abroad or use a requirement for repatriation of capital as a means of achieving exchange of information to the OECD standard by requiring repatriation only where the assets concealed are held in a jurisdiction beyond the scope of the AEoI (OECD 2015).

In contrast to tax amnestics—which arc discrctionary, temporary programs—voluntary disclosure programs are often part of the general law and valid for an unlimited period. They allow only individuals not yet under investigation for tax evasion to report all their foreign asset holdings. Under these programs, the income on these assets is then taxed retroactively at the standard tax rate, but either no or a reduced fine is imposed. Many countries incentivize individuals who have made intended or unintended errors in their tax strategy or inherited offshore accounts to come clean with "voluntary disclosure" programs. Langenmayr (2017), however, argues that the existence of a voluntary disclosure mechanism increases tax evasion. She predicts that if the detection probability increases due to a higher tax transparency, governments should increase the fine that applies after a voluntary disclosure to keep voluntary disclosure mechanism efficient.

3.2.3 Transfer to Nonbankable Assets

Nonbankable assets comprise, for example, **real** estate, mortgages, third party derivatives, art collections, airplanes, and yachts. Nonbankable assets can be held by a foundation or trust or managed by a private label fund.

Private label funds are collective investment vehicles for one or more investors. The private label funds are offered by universal banks, they are managed by a professional fund administer and, depending on the jurisdiction, the assets are managed by a licensed investment manager. Due to the private nature of the fund, it is generally under no or only light supervision, but it operates in a regulated environment. A private label fund can offer several advantages, e.g., it allows a consolidation of all assets and accounts in one vehicle, the investors gain increased access to larger investment transactions, it enhances privacy by segregating the assets from personal ownership, and furthermore it may offer a tax deferral depending on the investor's country of residence or potentially other tax benefits, e.g., stamp tax exemption.

Due to the diverse options to structure and manage nonbankable assets, the transfer from bankable to nonbankable assets creates new opportunities in cross-border wealth management and enhances portfolio diversification. Although the transfer creates costs, they may be compensated by the opportunities that nonbankable assets offer.

4 Factors That Impact on Cross-Border Wealth Management Structures

4.1 Risks

4.1.1 Currency Risk

In many cases (though not in all), cross-border wealth management also involves multiple currencies, which may entail currency risk. At the corporate level, currency risk is typically divided into transaction risk, translation risk, and economic risk (Levy 2009). For the investor, translation risk and economic risk are typically most relevant. Translation risk arises whenever the investor is ultimately concerned about his wealth when measured in a particular currency. In wealth management, this may or may not be a major issue: in the case of a family office, investments in both Europe and the USA create translation risk if all family members live either on one or the other side of the Atlantic—if the places of residence of family members are split, and this split corresponds to their share in the total portfolio, translation risk may be (almost) eliminated. A similar reasoning applies to an individual investor, who regularly spends part of the year in one region and the rest in another.

Economic risk describes an indirect effect of changes in exchange rates, i.e., fluctuations in asset values due to their dependence on gains and losses, which in turn depend on exchange rates. For example, Swiss exporters were affected by the strengthening of the Swiss franc in recent years, because sales abroad went down, either by a need to decrease prices to remain competitive or by a decrease in volume (or a combination of both). Economic risk arises always when investing in a different currency area. The different currency risk categories play an important role when it comes to risk management: whereas translation risk can, at least in theory, be perfectly hedged (albeit at a cost), economic risk cannot. Since taking on currency risk yields risk premia that are negligible at best, the benefits of such investments must come purely from the arguments discussed in Sect. 2: international diversification and locational advantages.

4.1.2 Political Risk

In times of increasing uncertainty and political instability worldwide, the role of political risk in cross-border wealth management differs markedly from previous decades. Not only has the number of conflicts and the number of people affected by them grown, but also the spectrum of political risks has changed. Investors basically have two possibilities to react: to tilt their portfolios toward stable countries to reduce political risk or take on political risk consciously (in which case diversification is advisable). Stability is typically an important factor when it comes to storing mobile assets (which includes financial securities, precious metals, and the like), for the choice of the place of residency, and for the location of the centralized wealth management. Given the wide range of political risks, its different aspects have to be considered separately, depending on the decision at hand. Whereas countries like China may be regarded as relatively low risk for civil war and terrorism and therefore interesting for corporate investments, legal risks regarding personal wealth make them uninteresting as places of residence or the location for centralized wealth management.

4.1.3 Legal Certainty

From a legal point of view, cross-border wealth management structures are influenced from a risk as well as from a cost perspective. Political risk as described from an economic point of view also comprises aspects of the legal environment and legal certainty.

There are two prerequisites for cross-border wealth management from a legal point of view. On the one hand, the legal environment of the respective countries must permit access of the relevant natural and legal persons to the home market, and they must be recognized legally. On the other hand, the relevant jurisdictions must offer sufficient legal certainty that the involved parties dare to go cross-border. Both questions depend on legal policy considerations that go far beyond a specific financial structure or intermediary and usually lie not in the sphere of influence of the participating parties.

Legal certainty is an essential feature of a state under the rule of law. It depends on various factors such as legal clarity and protection of legitimate expectations of individuals. [14] In order to provide legal certainty, a jurisdiction must provide a well-functioning legal system and independent jurisprudence. Legal uncertainty constitutes a legal risk/political risk in cross-border wealth management. The predictability of state activity and the possibility to enforce contractual rights must be considered when choosing target countries for cross-border wealth management. At the same time, the absence of those principles is often the reason for wealthy individuals to take their wealth to a foreign jurisdiction, hence across the border.

[14] See for the German GG Maunz, T., Dürig, G., & Herzog, R. (Eds.) (2013). Grundgesetz: Kommentar. (München: Beck-Online), Art. 20, Rn. 50.; for the Swiss BV see Ehrenzeller, B. (Ed.) (2008). Die schweizerische Bundesverfassung: Kommentar. (Zürich: Dike) and Art. 5, Rn. 4.; for the Austrian B-VG.

4.2 Multilateral Agreements and Regulatory Competition

The convergence and interaction between the respective national laws is a major source of influence for cross-border wealth management. It reduces legal costs and risks of cross-border wealth management significantly. Convergence of national laws happens either through multilateral treaties between two or more jurisdictions or through voluntary alignment of the national legislation of one country to the legislation of another. Voluntary alignment is mostly based on the wish not to be excluded from an important target market because of a lower or different regulatory standard. [15] We call it harmonization of law.

Harmonization of law is both a driver and prerequisite for the elimination of borders between jurisdictions in financial markets. And it's a game changer with respect to regulatory competition. Multilateral agreements address the tension between protection of the home market against outside competition or risk and the enhancement of competition and more liquid, larger, and deeper markets. [16] These aspects are of course not unique for financial services.

4.2.1 Elimination of Borders (Passporting)

Barriers between jurisdictions can be overcome through individual authorization by national authorities. The access to authorization however depends on political considerations of jurisdictions involved. These factors, such as the reciprocity of market access, are beyond influence by the individual service provider or investor. But even if an individual authorization process is available, the procedures can be costly and onerous and establish a factual barrier for cross-border wealth management.

The first step toward the elimination of borders is the guarantee of nondiscriminative market access for all foreign intermediaries. Multilateral agreements on the liberalization of financial services aim to provide this access by means of cross-border flow of services, the consumption of services in another member state, and the territorial presence of service providers in other member states. [17] As such the global general agreement on trade in services (GATS), entered into force in 1995, is also relevant for the financial services sector. [18] For intermediaries of all contracting parties, the treatment must be no less favorable than to one of any other participating

[15] See Zetzsche, D. (2014). "Drittstaaten" im Europäischen Bank-und Finanzmarktrecht. In B. G., & B. Breig (Eds.), *Finanzmarktregulierung zwischen Innovation und Kontinuität* (pp. 48–140). Tübingen: Mohr Siebeck.

[16] See ibid.; Warner, E. W. (1992). Mutual recognition" and cross-border financial services in the European community. *Law and Contemporary Problems*, 55(4), 7–28; European Commission (2015) 'SWD(2015) 183 final (Commission Staff Working Paper - Impact Assessment)'. Available at: http://eur-lex.europa.eu/legal-content/EN/TXT/PDF/?uri=CELEX:52015SC0183&from=en

[17] See, e.g., Art. 1 para 2 GATS Agreement.

[18] See Annex on financial services.

country (most-favored-nation treatment). [19] Preferential treatment of intermediaries of specific partner jurisdictions versus others or the requirement for reciprocity is not allowed. This of course promotes common standards for the authorization of foreign intermediaries and a more transparent regulation of market access.

The European Economic Area of course takes the elimination of borders a few steps further. The European Union establishes an internal market that is an "area without internal frontiers." [20] The treaty of the functioning of the European Union (TFEU) provides for four fundamental freedoms: the free movement of goods, persons, services, and capital. [21] In the context of cross-border wealth management, the free movement of capital also covers cross-border investments in undertakings as shareholder, buying securities on capital markets, acquiring control, and managing a company in a cross-border context. [22] Acquiring controlling stakes in companies is also covered by the right of establishment of Art. 49 TFEU. [23] This abolition of trade barriers is called negative integration (Hertig 2000, p. 352).

Over and above the most-favored-nation treatment principle, the access of other member state's individuals must be comparable to that of domestic market participants. European regulation is based on home control and the principle of mutual recognition. Due to the setting of collective minimum standards, it is anticipated that the regulatory standards within the European Union are adequate. A restriction of cross-border activities may thus only be restricted in exceptional cases in order to protect the public good. [24]

A further step in the elimination of border in financial services law constitutes the introduction of the so-called "European passport" for financial services. Following intensive harmonization of laws within the EEA, financial intermediaries and products may, after being authorized in one single member state, establish a branch, provide services, or be sold to market participants in the whole EEA. [25]

---

[19] Art. 2 GATS Agreement.

[20] Art. 26 (1) TFEU.

[21] Art. 26 (2) TFEU.

[22] See Commission Communication (2005). Intra-EU investment in the financial services` sector. https://eur-lex.europa.eu/legal-content/EN/TXT/PDF/?uri=CELEX:52005XC1125(01)&from=EN

[23] See Commission Communication (2005, Nr. 2).

[24] See Haar, B. (2015). Organising regional systems: The EU example. In N. Moloney, E. Ferran, & J. Payne (Eds.), *The Oxford handbook of financial regulation* (pp. 158–183). Oxford: Oxford University Press; Buttigieg, C. P. (2015). Governance of securities regulation and supervision: Quo vadis Europa. *Columbia Journal of European Law*, 21(3), 411–449.

[25] Art. 33 et seq CRD; Art. 32 et seq AIFMD; Art. 91 et seq. UCITSD; Art. 34 et seq MIFID II.

4.2.2 European and Global Harmonization

Multilateral agreements on the liberalization of financial services aim to provide nondiscriminative market access or, in the case of the EEA, even as much as mutual recognition (negative integration). They depend, however, on the harmonization of laws (positive integration) (Hertig 2000, p. 352). Opening the domestic market for foreign intermediaries requires trust in their regulation and supervision in the respective home member state (Buttigieg 2015, p. 414). Market and investor protection standards must therefore be comparable between the member states. The harmonization of financial markets law within Europe, but also globally, has gained momentum during the last decade. After the financial crisis, the G20 declared their common principles for a financial market reform, which include that all financial markets, products, and market participants should be regulated and subject to supervision (G20 2008, p. 3).

Harmonization of Law

Harmonization of law may be achieved in various ways from bi- or multilateral agreements to legally nonbinding model laws or model contracts. [26] The harmonization of law may have various intensities. Depending on the kind of legal act and the level of harmonization, member states have only limited flexibility in the transposition and application of financial services law. The extent of harmonization of course is based on political and economic considerations. Both politics and financial markets have changed significantly since the creation of the European Economic Area.

Minimum harmonization aims at the creation of a common ground and a basic level of trust between the participating member states to enable cross-border business. In the Treaty of Rome, the contracting parties establishing the European Economic Community once decided for an "approximation" of laws to the extent required for the proper functioning of the common market. [27] Little did they know that the proper functioning of the financial market within the European union would, in light of the financial crisis, require a set of highly complex and very detailed regulatory acts that leave only little leeway for diversity. This trend toward maximum harmonization is illustrated by the recently more frequent use of regulations rather than directives in European financial regulation. [28]

However, in particular, in light of the principle of subsidiarity within the European Union, minimum harmonization still has its place. In the EEA, we experience today a combination of maximum and minimum harmonization (quasi-maximum harmonization) (Buttigieg 2015, p. 422). The former is used when market protection and

[26] See Goode, R. (1991). Reflections on the Harmonisation of Commercial Law *Uniform Law Review*, 19(1), 54–74. https://doi.org/10.1093/ulr/os-19.1.54

[27] Art. 3 lit. h) Treaty of Rome, 25 March 1957.

[28] See CRR, MFIR, EMIR, and the extensive level 2 legislative acts in the field of alternative investment funds.

financial stability require a consistent set of rules (single rule book); the latter is used when flexibility is justified.

Harmonization of Supervision

Financial supervision protects the stability and integrity of the markets and the investor. Besides a harmonization on a regulatory level and therefore in the letters of law, global harmonization of financial supervision, meaning the fine print in regulation, is necessary. Harmonization is not only necessary when it comes to discretion of national supervisory authorities under harmonized regulation but also and even more importantly with respect to the interpretation of legal stipulations. Supervisory convergence in a cross-border context requires communication and cooperation between national supervisory bodies, in order to prevent regulatory arbitrage and provide for a consistent application of rules also in a cross-border context.

Effective macro-prudential oversight over financial institutions requires also harmonization of financial supervision. There are various ways how this harmonization may be achieved. And they are located between the poles of national sovereignty and supranational cooperation. In order to truly harmonize supervision, you would need a central supranational supervisory authority with the right to intervene on the level of the subordinate domestic supervisory. Obviously, this is difficult to implement from a political perspective due to strong interference with national sovereignty (Chiodini and Ferrarini 2012, p. 194). Alternatively, harmonization of supervision may happen through various kinds of cooperation between national supervisory authorities (Chiodini and Ferrarini 2012, p. 194).

Within the European Union, middle road between supranationality and national sovereignty is achieved through mixed system of financial supervision. The European System of Financial Supervision (ESFS) is mainly decentralized and multilayered. The primary supervisory responsibility is allocated to the national supervisory authorities (NSAs), whereas the European Supervisory Authorities' (ESAs) role is mainly of a coordinating nature with respect to cross-border and cross-sectoral harmonization. The ESRB, as a truly supranational body that carries out macro-prudential oversight, is restricted to assessment and monitoring and the issuance of warnings and recommendations. In specific areas, however, the ESAs assume direct supervisory tasks. This is true for the supervision of intermediaries with a very strong cross-border activity such as credit rating agencies and trade repositories. [29]

From the perspective of the financial intermediary, harmonized supervision may be advantageous, because in a cross-border context, actions of foreign supervisory authorities become more predictable. On the other hand, however, financial intermediaries may get in touch with a domestic regulator more easily and therefore may

[29] E.g. Art. 16 et seq. CRAR, Art. 55 et seq. EMIR.

benefit from a little leeway on the national level (Chiodini and Ferrarini 2012, p. 194).

4.3 Regulatory Competition

The possibility to go cross-border and engage in regulatory arbitrage leads to regulatory competition. It is based on the idea that the legal environment and institutional characteristics influence the amount of capital that can be attracted from abroad (Buttigieg 2015, p. 413; European Commission 2015, p. 71). The economic analysis of law suggests that political agency costs may be mitigated through regulatory competition and lead to greater efficiency. [30] In light of the complexity of regulatory endeavors, the public good that regulation of financial markets protects, and the interconnectedness of the financial system, this conclusion is, however, shortsighted. [31]

Progressing global harmonization of course limits the possibilities for regulatory arbitrage and regulatory competition. However, even after several years of extensive vertical and horizontal harmonization in European financial services law, regulatory competition is alive and well. This has three reasons: mobility, complexity, and enforcement. First, competition is intensified due to the higher comparability of regulation and the higher mobility of intermediaries and products. Second, regulatory arbitrage and thus competition is not limited to harmonized financial regulation, but also to improperly harmonized law, such as company law, civil liability, enforcement of contracts, or insolvency law. [32] Third, general norms may be possible to harmonize, but the harmonization supervision is an entirely different matter (see above).

The question as to which extent regulatory competition is possible under EU law is to be separated from the question as to which extent national regulators are constitutionally empowered to engage in regulatory competition. Regulators protect a public interest and in this function are constitutionally restricted to achieve specific regulatory goals. In the case of financial regulation, these goals are the protection of investors and the financial market. Whether regulatory competition is covered depends on how wide the "functioning of the financial market" may be understood and whether regulators may support the markets competitiveness by way of regulation. The Swiss FINMAG finds the most liberal wording in this context, when it prompts the financial market supervision to contribute to "sustaining the reputation and competitiveness of Switzerland's financial centre." [33] However, in this case,

---

[30] With respect to choice of law systems, see O'Hara O'Connor, E. A., and Ribstein, L. (2000). From politics to efficiency in choice of law. *University of Chicago Law Review*, 67(4), 1151–1232.

[31] See Buttigieg (2015, p. 413).

[32] See European Commission (2015, pp. 71–77); for company law, see Hopt (2015, p. 164).

[33] Art. 5 FINMAG.

engaging in regulatory competition by deregulation in the short term is restricted by the goal of maintaining financial centers reputation in the long haul. Also, in the EEA, the discretionary powers of supervisory authorities should only be used to protect the interest for which those powers were foreseen. [34]

4.4 *Taxation*

The international and European tax law has changed significantly over the last 25 years. Whereas the laws of indirect taxes have been largely harmonized within the European Union (EU), the direct taxation laws have not been influenced by the EU prior to the 1990 Directives that entered into force. In the subsequent years, the European Court of Justice has influenced income taxation of cross-border investment and activities by activating the fundamental freedoms. In the recent past, additional policies and measures aimed to achieve intra-European tax neutrality, as the European Commission's Action Plan for a Fair and Efficient Tax System, the facilitation of cross-border administrative assistance, the Base Erosion and Profit Shifting (BEPS) Action Plan, and the EU Anti-Tax Avoidance Directives (ATAD I and II) as part of the EU Anti-Tax Avoidance Package (ATAP).

4.4.1 From BEPS to ATAD

Subsequent to the G20/OECD's Base Erosion and Profit Shifting (BEPS) project, the European Commission (EC) launched an Anti-Tax Avoidance Package (ATAP). The Anti-Tax Avoidance Directives (ATAD I and II) are part of the ATAP. The agreement requires all member states to enact laws that largely implement BEPS outcomes on interest limitation rules, hybrid mismatches, and controlled foreign companies (CFCs) as well as additional measures on exit taxation and a general anti-abuse rule (GAAR). Whereas the topics exit taxation and GAAR are not covered by the BEPS project, the switchover clause to require a tax credit rather an exemption on certain income, which would have provided a minimum effective tax rate, was dropped as part of the compromise agreement.

As the member states should apply these measures apart from January 1, 2019, and 2020, respectively, the directive creates a "level playing field" throughout the EU. However, the ATAD I and II may have a bigger impact in those member states that have currently no CFC rules (which concerns about half of the 28 EU member states). The CFC rules aim to deter profit shifting to a low or no tax country. This would be achieved by reattributing nondistributed income of low-taxed CFC, which is not a publicly listed company, to its parent company. The switchover rule prevents double nontaxation of certain income by taxing, for example, dividends coming into

[34] See Commission Communication (2005, Nr. 1).

the EU, if they have not already been properly taxed in a third country. Exit taxation aims to prevent companies from avoiding tax when relocating assets. In doing so, the market value (arm's length) of the asset involved in the transfer minus the tax value is to be taxed when a taxpayer transfers assets, its tax residence, or its PE out of a member state. The interest limitation aims to discourage artificial debt arrangements designed to minimize taxes. The GAAR aims to counteract aggressive tax planning when other rules do not apply. This enables tax authorities to ignore "wholly artificial arrangements" where the essential purpose is to obtain a tax advantage. The tax liability would then be "calculated in accordance with national law."

The ATAD I and II are a midterm aim of the EC's tax policy. The ultimate goal is the Common Consolidated Corporate Tax Base (CCCTB). The CCCTB is a set of common rules for determining the taxable profits of companies with operations in several EU member states, based on International Financial Reporting Standards (IFRS). The aggregated profits will be apportioned between member states on an agreed basis. Finally, every allotted share of profit is taxed in the respective member state with the relevant corporate tax rate. This tax base harmonization may facilitate cross-border activities within the EEA. On the other hand, however, the standardization limits the diversity and innovative capacity of tax systems.

4.4.2 Tax Cooperation and Tax Transparency

A fundamental prerequisite in international tax cooperation is an effective exchange of information. Since 1971, when the OECD established its Working Party on Tax Avoidance and Evasion, an enormous progress has been made to implement high standards of tax transparency and to facilitate exchange of information so as to improve tax authorities' ability to deter, detect, and disrupt tax evasion and avoidance (OECD 2016).

Information exchange can be achieved by various forms, ranging from information exchange on request to spontaneous and automatic exchange of information (AEoI). An AEoI is a systematic and periodic transmission of tax information by financial institutions (i.e., banks, insurance companies, and certain investment companies) concerning customers (individuals and companies) with a tax domicile in a different country than the financial institution (cross-border perspective). The AEoI concerns various categories of income, such as dividends, interest, gross proceeds, royalties, salaries, and pensions. For purposes of whether or where the information has to be submitted, the actual beneficial owners of the account have to be identified. This means that passive structures, such as foundations, trusts, or domicile companies, will be treated transparently under the AEoI.

Up to today, about 100 jurisdictions have now committed to implement the AEoI standard, with exchanges beginning in 2017 and 2018. In the run-up, almost 55 billion USD in additional tax revenues generated through voluntary disclosure programs and similar measures aimed to encourage taxpayers to report previously non-declared income and wealth (OECD 2016).

With regard to cross-border wealth management, the common reporting standard (CRS) will minimize the compliance burdens for both financial institutions and governments. Additionally, the international exchange of information is facilitated by CRS Multilateral Competent Authority Agreement (CRS MCAA), which specifies the details of what information will be exchanged and when. The CRS MCAA is signed up to date by 87 countries, among them Liechtenstein, Germany, (which started the first information exchange by September 2017), Austria, and Switzerland (started by September 2018). Furthermore, it will increase voluntary compliance, as the regularization of untaxed assets prior to the introduction of the AEoI is highly recommended, if not the only possibility to prevent criminal prosecution.

5 Conclusion

In general, empirical evidence on cross-border wealth management is scarce. This is mainly due to the (understandable) reluctance on the part of investors and investment managers (such as family offices) to disclose information. Whereas anonymized data on retail investors can be made available more easily without any risk of making investors in the dataset identifiable individually, the data on high-net-worth individuals are much more sensitive in this regard. Nevertheless, we could learn a lot from having more and better data on wealth management to analyze. This includes information on investors' motivation for making certain decisions, which could only be gathered from interview with investors and/or managers. Not surprisingly, this type of information is even more difficult to obtain.

References

Achkar R (2016) OTC derivatives under MiFID II - transparency only through collaboration. http://www.derivalert.org/blog/bid/108815/OTC-Derivatives-Under-MiFID-II-Transparency-Only-Through-Collaboration Accessed 2 April 2016

Arner DA, Avgouleas E, Buckley RP (eds) (2016) Reconceptualising global finance and its regulation. Cambridge University Press, Cambridge

Arnott RD, Berkin AL, Ye J (2001) Loss harvesting: what's it worth to the taxable investor? J Wealth Manag 3(4):10–18

Bader D, Bär A, Leu D (2015) Single family Offices in der Schweiz. Aktuelle juristische Praxis - Pratique juridique Actuelle 24(7):979–992

Berkin AL, Ye J (2003) Tax management, loss harvesting, and HIFO accounting. Financ Anal J 59(4):91–102

Borg Barthet J (2010) A new approach to the governing law of companies in the EU: a legislative proposal. J Priv Int Law 6(3):589–621

Bösch H 2/15 (2015) Unklarheiten im Zusammenhang mit liechtensteinischen Trusts in der Schweiz (BGer 4A_329/2013): Versuch einer Wegleitung. http://kanzleiboesch.com/files/kanzlei-boesch/Publikationen/PDF/Download_Unklarheiten_iZm_liechtensteinischen_Trusts_in_der_Schweiz.pdf

Butterstein A (2015) Die Rechtsprechung als Vehikel nationaler Kontrolle über die Harmonisierung des internationalen Gesellschaftsrechts am Beispiel der liechtensteinschen Stiftung. In: Nueber M, Przeszlowska D, Michael Z (eds) Privatautonomie und ihre Grenzen im Wandel. Verl. Österreich, Wien, p 3
Buttigieg CP (2015) Governance of securities regulation and supervision: Quo vadis Europa. Columbia J Eur Law 21(3):411–449
Chincarini LB, Kim D (2001) The advantages of tax-managed investing. J Portf Manag 28(1):56–72
Chiodini F, Ferrarini GA (2012) Nationally fragmented supervision over multinational banks as a source of global systemic risk: a critical analysis of recent EU reforms. In: Wymeersch E, Hopt KJ, Ferrarini G (eds) Financial regulation and supervision: a post-crisis analysis. Oxford Oxford University Press. https://doi.org/10.2139/ssrn.1923756
Christensen H, Tirard JM (2016) The amazing development of exchange of information in tax matters: from double tax treaties to FATCA and the CRS. Trusts Trustees 22(8):898–922
Christoffersen S, Geczy C, Musto D, Reed A (2005) Crossborder dividend taxation and the preferences of taxable and nontaxable investors: evidence from Canada. J Financ Econ 78(1):121–144
Coates W (1924) League of nations report on double taxation submitted to the financial committee by Professors Bruins, Einaudi, Seligman, and Sir Josiah Stamp. J R Stat Soc 87(1):99–102
Commission Communication (2005) Intra-EU investment in the financial services' sector. https://eur-lex.europa.eu/legal-content/EN/TXT/PDF/?uri=CELEX:52005XC1125(01)&from=EN
Ehrenzeller B (ed) (2008) Die schweizerische Bundesverfassung: Kommentar. Dike, Zürich
Eidenmüller H (2011) The transnational law market, regulatory competition, and transnational corporations. Indiana J Glob Leg Stud 18(2):707–749
Ernst & Young (2015) Automatic exchange of information: the challenges to get it right. https://webforms.ey.com/lu/en/newsroom/pr-activities/articles/article_20150105_automatic_exchange_of_information
European Commission (2012) SWD(2012) 387 final (Commission Staff Working Paper - Impact Assessment). http://ec.europa.eu/smart-regulation/impact/ia_carried_out/docs/ia_2012/swd_2012_0386_en.pdf
European Commission (2015) SWD(2015) 183 final (Commission Staff Working Paper - Impact Assessment). http://eur-lex.europa.eu/legal-content/EN/TXT/PDF/?uri=CELEX:52015SC0183&from=en
European Commission (2016) Parent companies and their subsidiaries in the European Union. https://ec.europa.eu/taxation_customs/business/company-tax/parent-companies-their-subsidiaries-eu-union_en
Family Office Council (2015) Defining 'Family office'. https://familyofficecouncil.com/the-family-office/. Accessed 10 April 2016
Fazzi R (2005) Defining wealth management. https://www.fa-mag.com/news/article-1172.html. Accessed 10 April 2016
Fleischer V (2010) Regulatory arbitrage. Texas Law Rev 89(2):227–290
French KR, Poterba JM (1991) Investor diversification and international equity markets. Am Econ Rev 81(2):222–226
Friedlander R (2015) Transparency: five years after the Dodd-Frank Act. https://www.treasury.gov/connect/blog/Pages/Transparency. Accessed 10 April 2016
G20 (2008) Declaration of the summit on financial markets and the world economy
Goode R (1991) Reflections on the harmonisation of commercial law. Unif Law Rev 19(1):54–74. https://doi.org/10.1093/ulr/os-19.1.54
Haar B (2015) Organising regional systems: the EU example. In: Moloney N, Ferran E, Payne J (eds) The Oxford handbook of financial regulation. Oxford University Press, Oxford, pp 158–183
Hertig G (2000) Regulatory competition for EU financial services. J Int Econ Law 3(2):349–375. https://doi.org/10.1093/jiel/3.2.349

Höhn N, Höring J (2010) Das Steuerrecht international agierender Unternehmen: Grenzüberschreitende Steuerplanung. Gabler Verlag/Springer Fachmedien Wiesbaden GmbH, Wiesbaden
Hopt KJ (2015) Corporate governance in Europe: a critical review of the European Commission's initiatives on corporate law and corporate governance. N Y Univ J Law Bus 12(1):139–213
Horvitz JE, Wilcox JW (2003) Know when to hold 'em and when to fold 'em: the value of effective taxable investment management. J Wealth Manag 6(2):35–59
International Monetary Fund (2008) Global financial stability report: containing systemic risks and restoring financial stability. http://www.imf.org/External/Pubs/FT/GFSR/2008/01/index.htm. Accessed 9 April 2016
Jacob D, Studen G (2016) Swiss family foundations and the new registration requirement: paper tiger or paradigm shift? Trusts Trustees 22(6):707–712
Jennings WW, Horan SM, Reichenstein W, Brunel JL (2011) Perspectives from the literature of private wealth management. J Wealth Manag 14(1):8–40
Kozey SJ (2015) The Hague securities convention: an opportunity to take the UCC global. Georgetown J Int Law 46(4):1214–1244
Lambert P (2016) Focus on wealth management: tax transparency and cross-border activity. https://www.scoperatings.com/study/download-mail?id=f3a95190-47ce-4162-aadf-35bc2b0bed60. Accessed 5 April 2018
Langenmayr D (2017) Voluntary disclosure of evaded taxes: increasing revenue, or increasing incentives to evade? J Public Econ 151(C):110–125
Levy MD (2009) International finance. Routledge, New York
Lissi A, Utzinger MG (2016) Swiss witholding tax in collective investment schemes. http://www.internationaltaxreview.com/Article/3569924/Swiss-withholding-tax-in-collective-investment-schemes.html. Accessed 9 January 2017
Markowitz HM (1952) Portfolio selection. J Financ 7(1):77–91
Markowitz HM (1970) Portfolio analysis: efficient diversification of investments. Yale University Press, London
Marschner E (2015) Optimierung der Familienstiftung: Aus der Sicht der Begünstigten. Linde, Wien
Maunz T, Dürig G, Herzog R (eds) (2013) Grundgesetz: Kommentar. Beck-Online, Munich
Morgan G, Thorum M (2016) Determinants of transnational regulatory regimes
Mosely L, Singer DA (2009) The global financial crisis: lessons and opportunities for international political economy. Int Interact 35(4):420–429
O'Hara EA, Ribstein L (2000) From politics to efficiency in choice of law. Univ Chicago Law Rev 67(4):1151–1232
Odier P, Solnik B (1993) Lessons for international asset allocation. Financ Anal J 49(2):63–77
OECD (1999) Taxation of cross-border portfolio investment: mutual funds and possible tax distortions. Paris. https://doi.org/10.1787/9789264172883-en
OECD (2015) Update on voluntary disclosure programmes: a pathway to tax compliances. Offshore Voluntary Disclosure Programmes Publication. https://www.oecd.org/ctp/exchange-of-ta
OECD (2016) Secretary-general report to G20 leaders. https://www.oecd.org/tax/oecd-secretary-general-tax-report-g20-leaders-september-2016.pdf. Accessed 5 April 2018
Rammeloo S (2003) The long and winding road towards freedom of establishment for legal persons in Europe. Maastricht J Eur Comp Law 10(2):169–197
Rogers JS (2006) Conflict of laws for transactions in securities held through intermediaries. Cornell Int Law J 39(2):285–328
Sialm C, Starks L, Zhang H (2015) Defined contribution pension plans: sticky or discerning money? J Financ 70(2):805–838
Stein DM, Narasimhan P (1999) Of passive and active equity portfolios in the presence of taxes. J Wealth Manag 2(2):55–63
Tesar LL, Werner IM (1995) Home bias and high turnover. J Int Money Financ 14(4):467–492
Thaler RH (1985) Mental accounting and consumer choice. Mark Sci 4(3):199–214

Thévenoz L (2013) The Geneva securities convention: objectives, history, and guiding principles. In: Thévenoz L, Conac P-H, Segna U (eds) Intermediated securities: the impact of the Geneva securities convention and the future European legislation. Cambridge University Press, Cambridge, pp 3–21

Vogenauer S (2013) Regulatory competition in contract law and dispute resolution. In: Eidenmüller H (ed) Regulatory competition through choice of contract law and forum in Europe: theory and evidence. Beck, Munich, pp 240–297

Warner EW (1992) "Mutual recognition" and cross-border financial services in the European community. Law Contemp Probl 55(4):7–28

Zetzsche D (2014) "Drittstaaten" im Europäischen Bank-und Finanzmarktrecht. In: Bachmann G, Breig B (eds) Finanzmarktregulierung zwischen Innovation und Kontinuität. Mohr Siebeck, Tübingen, pp 48–140

Zetzsche D (2016) Competitiveness of financial centers in light of financial and tax law equivalence requirements. In: Buckley E, Avgouleas E, Arner DW (eds) Reconceptualising global finance and its regulation. Cambridge University Press, Cambridge, pp 390–418

Crowdfunding in German-Speaking Countries: A Literature Review from an Economics and Legal Perspective

Martin Angerer, Sascha Kraus, and Andreas Peter

Abstract A solid amount of research on crowdfunding per se is available; however, cross-border issues remain largely neglected. Although crowdfunding campaigns are theoretically easy to establish over the Internet, projects with their origin in small countries such as Liechtenstein constantly face the limitation of potential financing within a country with only a few people and therefore have only minor investment potential. We use a systematic literature review to analyze and build on well-known success factors, to identify three key factors to consider when targeting cross-border investors—behavioral biases, multiple taxation system, and multiple legislation—which are approached in a multidisciplinary discussion.

1 Introduction

Start-up funding is a fundamental step for entrepreneurs when they're establishing their venture (Metzger 2015). Entrepreneurs generally have several traditional options for obtaining necessary funding from capital sources. However, banks, public funding, venture capital firms, and other investors often only insufficiently support young ventures (Beck 2017). There is even evidence of an early *funding gap* in the start-up finance market (Hemer 2011). Because funding is essential when it comes to avoiding start-up failure (Yallapragada and Bhuiyan 2011), the relatively new concept of crowdfunding can be an alternative for funding start-ups through external finance (along with the projects of existing successful firms) (Hornuf and Schwienbacher 2015). While it is so far still considered a niche phenomenon, compared to the overall capital markets, money collected by crowdfunding is notably

M. Angerer (✉) · A. Peter
University of Liechtenstein, Vaduz, Liechtenstein
e-mail: martin.angerer@uni.li

S. Kraus
Free University of Bozen-Bolzano, Bolzano, Italy
e-mail: Sascha.Kraus@unibz.it

P. Droege et al. (eds.), *Cross-Border Life and Work*, Contributions to Management Science, https://doi.org/10.1007/978-3-031-34362-9_5

expanding (Belleflamme et al. 2015). In February 2014, the computer game "Star Citizen" collected about 72 million USD through crowdfunding. This kind of example illustrates that crowdfunding might have the potential to narrow the early-stage funding gap (The Economist 2015). Capital here is generally invested by "the crowd" to obtain a financial or nonfinancial return, which can even be intangible (Ordanini et al. 2011).

Crowdfunding is the general term for several divergent types of funding schemes (Ahlers et al. 2015). The crowdfunding market is divided into four distinguishable types of capital collection: donation, reward, equity, and lending-based crowdfunding. In our article, we will focus primarily on *equity crowdfunding* because it is currently the fastest growing approach in German-speaking countries. Here, investors receive equity or equity-like hybrid stakes in a start-up in return for their invested money (Klöhn and Hornuf 2012). In German-speaking countries, the term *crowdinvesting* is predominantly used instead (Kortleben and Vollmar 2012). Expanding the investment opportunities for noninstitutional investors, crowdfunding at the same time improves access to financial sources for start-ups (European Securities and Markets Authority 2014). The performance-sharing component of crowd investment allows investors to participate in the positive development of a firm (Beck 2017). Germany in particular has a vibrant crowdinvesting market because of its comparatively liberal equity crowdfunding legislation (Klöhn et al. 2016). The relevance of this topic is demonstrated by the fact that 64 out of 264 members of the Federal Association of German Start-Ups (*Bundesverband Deutsche Startups*) had used crowdinvesting by the end of 2014 (Blaseg and Koetter 2015).

An important question, especially for smaller countries, is how *cross-border crowdfunding* projects can be successfully established; which regulations need to be fulfilled; and what the important legal, behavioral, and economic factors are. The four-country region of Liechtenstein, Germany, Switzerland, and Austria provides a particularly insightful environment for comparing the current situation as a first step toward answering this question. These four countries share the same culture, language, level of computer literacy, wealth, Internet coverage, and legal tradition. They are described in the literature as "German-civil law countries." Moreover, in the world value graph and other ethical studies (keeping in mind that these do not share every single value), the four countries are quite close together, allowing us to believe that ethics as an alternative factor of crowdfunding plays a minor role. We deem this regional setup as a nearly perfect environment for studying the impact of borders.

A number of authors point out the need for additional studies on the topic of successful equity crowdfunding. First of all, it is still unclear why start-ups actually *select* crowdinvesting as a funding source. Belleflamme et al. (2014) recommend future research on this question, arguing that there could be other reasons apart from capital collection that influence entrepreneurs to choose crowdfunding. Also, the main question arises about how start-ups are able to collect funding most successfully. This requires an understanding of the individual funders' investment behavior and determinants in greater detail (Crosetto and Regner 2014). Moritz and Block (2014) recommend for future research an identification of the quality signals which determine a backer's crowdfunding investment decision. The academic literature dealing with crowdfunding success factors mainly describes patterns from donation-, reward-, and lending-based crowdfunding (Hornuf and Neuenkirch 2015). Results from these types cannot be directly generalized to crowdinvesting because of the different characteristics of these funding models (Hornuf and Schwienbacher 2014a). This is why the existing literature focuses only on single success factors which are usually based on a study of one specific platform, neglecting cross-border characteristics. They also ignore crowdfunding processes before and after the funding campaign (Hornuf and Schwienbacher 2016). Hagedorn and Pinkwart (2013) have demonstrated that equity crowdfunding is more than the process of capital collection. It starts with the application and ends with the exit of the investor. Deffains-Crapsky and Sudolska (2014) recommend studying the investors' relation to the entrepreneur before and after the investors' investment decision. On the one hand, scholars point out that the existing scientific literature lacks studies which provide an understanding of why the entrepreneurs select crowdinvesting and how they can select capital in the most efficient way, also in regard to the pre- and post-funding period. On the other hand, there is no evidence on how the influence of legal, tax, and cultural borders can be minimized.

There is clearly an existing research gap regarding success factors for equity crowdfunding in German-speaking countries, most notably from a cross-border perspective.

2 Historical Development and Definitions of Crowdfunding

2.1 Origins of Crowdfunding

Dresner (2014) states that "crowdfunding is a new way to do something old" (p. 3). The idea of collecting money from a large amount of people existed prior to the Internet and is in fact a centuries-old approach (Hemer 2011). The construction of the Statue of Liberty in New York was, for example, funded by small donations from the citizens of France and the USA (Lawton et al. 2012). Crowdfunding however extended and altered this idea (Kortleben and Vollmar 2012). Traditional capital collection techniques, on the one hand, are mainly centrally organized activities with a regional and offline collection scheme. A limited passive supporter group is targeted through classical advertisement media which support the funding. Crowdfunding on the other hand is a purely online collection approach with decentralized activities with the potential for active supporters around the globe; it is mainly advertised through social media. These online social media platforms are used as intermediaries (Kortleben and Vollmar 2012). The idea of crowdfunding is deeply embedded in the concept of "crowdsourcing" (Belleflamme et al. 2014), a term coined by Surowiecki's (2005) description of "the wisdom of the crowd" which implies that in certain cases, group considerations and decisions are smarter and better compared to the results experts would provide in the same situation. When this is the case, it is not required that the average group member has a high degree of professionalism or intelligence. Crowdsourcing is actively conducted in business where a crowd offers its knowledge to solve or develop specific corporate tasks for a company, receiving some kind of benefit from its participation. The outsourcing company profits from a lower cost level and potentially better solutions (Beck 2017). Altogether, crowdsourcing can be described as a solution-based approach, while crowdfunding is based on a financially oriented approach.

The first worldwide crowdfunding platform was the US website *ArtistShare.com*. Since 2003, backers have had the opportunity to fund musicians on this platform (Kortleben and Vollmar 2012). Creative industries were largely the origin of the overall crowdfunding phenomenon (Agrawal et al. 2013). Crowdfunding experienced strong growth with the launch of the currently largest crowdfunding platforms *Indiegogo* and *Kickstarter* in 2008 and 2009. Both platforms offer rewards for crowd participation (Freedman and Nutting 2015). Germany's first crowdfunding platform *Startnext* was launched in 2010 (Beck 2017). Parallel to the rising number of platforms, the capital collected with crowdfunding has increased notably in the recent years, reaching a worldwide estimated financing volume of 16.2 billion USD in 2014 (Massolution 2015). Crowdfunding experienced an average annual growth rate of 76% between 2009 and 2013, with its leading markets in North America having 60% and Europe having 36% of the market volume (Wilson and Testoni 2014). The European crowdfunding market has generated €3 billion, with German projects receiving €140 million in 2014 (Wardrop et al. 2015). All in all, crowdfunding, although rooted in older developments, is a relatively new and worldwide phenomenon that continues to expand.

The most prominent crowdfunding definition is provided by Belleflamme et al. (2014) who define it as "an open call, mostly through the Internet, for the provision of financial resources either in the form of donation or in exchange for the future product or some form of reward to support initiatives for specific purposes" (p. 588). Bouncken et al. (2015) have compared this definition with others and concluded that on the whole "crowdfunding focuses on raising financial funding from the public, represented by a group of people, by using specific internet-based platforms" (p. 409).

2.2 *Definitions and Approaches*

This chapter provides an introduction to crowdsourcing, crowdfunding, and its development as well as its different types to provide a general understanding of the basic models on which equity crowdfunding is based.

Current literature usually categorizes crowdfunding into different models: donation-, reward-, lending-, and equity-based crowdfunding (Bradford 2012; Beck 2017). Varying in regard to their complexity, these categories also have different degrees of uncertainty for their investors and fundraisers (Wilson and Testoni 2014).

Further, the funded amounts differ widely. Projects as high as 100,000 USD and as low as 100 USD are present on crowdfunding platforms (Mollick 2014).

Backers receive no return or reward for their provided money in the *donation* model, which is also called the *patronage model* (Mollick 2014). *Donation crowdfunding* is also called *fan funding* because fans often use it to support their favorite bands or artists (Beck 2017). An exception to the no-return-on-capital premise can be acknowledgments, which can have a high emotional value for fans (Beck 2017). Belleflamme et al. (2015), however, argue that the campaigns mentioning the funder are considered *reward crowdfunding*, emphasizing how the division between donation and reward crowdfunding is not always clear. The reward model includes real nonmonetary rewards, commonly related to the project, for the financial supporters of the crowdfunding campaign (Bradford 2012). Examples are the opportunity for backers to meet the campaign initiators or the crediting of their names in a movie (Mollick 2014). In some cases, the rewards are of a progressive nature. There are several categories of rewards offered to the investors depending on how high the financial contribution is (Beck 2017). Rewards can also include a preordering option. Here, investors participate in a campaign and obtain in return the product being funded before its official sale or publication, often at a discounted price (Hemer 2011). Certain scholars use the term *preordering* instead of the term *reward-based crowdfunding* (e.g., Belleflamme et al. 2014). Projects which represent a one-time event with a low capital threshold are often found in the donation or the reward model (Mollick 2014). The third category is *crowdlending*, which denotes a credit system for crowdfunding projects. The investors do not receive a stake in the company, even though they are creditors (Beck 2017). Receiving predetermined interest rates, the investors furthermore benefit from the repayment of the credit at the end of the credit period (Hornuf and Schwienbacher 2015).

The *equity crowdfunding* model provides the contributing investors with stakes in the start-up for their invested capital (Bradford 2012). Historically, the term equity crowdfunding emerged in the USA (Beck 2017), whereas in the German-speaking countries, the term *crowdinvesting* is synonymously used (Kortleben and Vollmar 2012). Crowdinvesting can be defined as "a method of financing, whereby an entrepreneur sells a specified amount of equity or bond-like shares in a company to a group of (small) investors through an open call for funding on Internet-based platforms" (Ahlers et al. 2015). Equity crowdfunding is the only type of crowdfunding which includes this equity component (Bradford 2012).

A capital contribution toward a project is financially beneficial for the investors in two ways. First, the crowdinvestors profit from the accretion of the company. Second, the added value is generated through the start-up's profit distribution. Start-up stakes are in the form of either equity or hybrid capital (Klöhn et al. 2016; Beck 2017). Entrepreneurs in particular use crowdinvesting to collect larger capital amounts. Start-ups prefer to collect smaller funding with the profit-sharing mechanism of the reward-based model. European start-ups can clearly benefit from crowdinvesting since it is the crowdinvesting market leader, generating most of the equity crowdfunding market growth (Belleflamme et al. 2014; Wilson and Testoni 2014).

Reaching €82.6 million in continental Europe in 2014, crowdinvesting experienced an average growth rate of 116% per annum from 2012 to 2014 (Wardrop et al. 2015).

3 Crowdinvesting as the Main Approach in German-Speaking Countries

There are usually three main players involved in the crowdfunding process: fundraisers, investors, and platforms. Fundraisers initiate a funding campaign for their projects and ideas. Their aim is to collect sufficient funds from supporters to successfully complete a project. The funds needed for the start-up are in general the amount of capital required to initiate the company. The investors, or funders, are the crowd of people who invest in a certain project. They generally expect some kind of monetary or nonmonetary reward for their capital contribution. The crowdfunding platform connects the fundraisers' project with the investors' financial engagement. The interaction between these actors can be described as taking place within an equity crowdfunding process (Ordanini et al. 2011; Hagedorn and Pinkwart 2013; Belleflamme et al. 2015).

3.1 The Equity Crowdfunding (Crowdinvesting) Process

According to Hagedorn and Pinkwart (2013), the equity crowdfunding process typically includes seven steps which are summarized in Fig. 1. The lifecycle of crowdinvesting begins with the application, screening, as well as selection and contracting. It is followed by the funding, subscription, and holding phases. The investor to start-up relationship is thereafter terminated in the exit stage.

Start-ups first submit their business idea and detailed information to equity crowdfunding platforms. Second, the crowdinvesting platforms review the information and then decide whether to accept the application or not. Sometimes the specific crowd evaluation is also taken into account by the platform. Third, the start-up and platform negotiate in the case of a positive outcome the details and terms of the funding process. The parties eventually agree on a contract for future engagement. Here, two contrary interests for publication arise. On the one hand, the investor side demands sufficient information to overcome the information asymmetries which hamper the evaluation of the business idea (Beck 2017). On the other hand, the start-ups insist on the limitation of the disclosure of certain information. Specific

Fig. 1 Typical equity crowdfunding process (Adapted from Hagedorn and Pinkwart (2013, p. 22))

ideas are sometimes heavily dependent on their secrecy, so the risk of losing key advantages such as the first mover advantage could emerge for the start-up in this kind of situation. The imitation risk is especially high during the project period and the establishment of the start-up (Agrawal et al. 2013). Hemer (2011) points out that it is very difficult from a legal standpoint to arrange a nondisclosure agreement with every investor.

Fourth, a video created by the fundraisers describing their project is posted on the platform's webpage. Crowdinvestors now have access to the project details and can decide whether to invest in the start-up or not (Beck 2017). The timeframe of the funding period is limited. Generally, the duration of the project is between 2 weeks and several months (Hemer 2011). The project is financed if it has reached the funding threshold within the given time. This is the case if the investors are willing to pledge the required amount of capital to a specific project, also referred to as a *campaign* (Belleflamme et al. 2015). Start-ups as well as crowdinvesting platforms have a major interest in reaching the specified funding threshold, which is why strong marketing efforts are undertaken to support the funding (Hagedorn and Pinkwart 2013). Potential backers are able to access detailed project information, including the campaign's current funding level (Kuppuswamy and Bayus 2013) and the number of backers who to date pledge capital to a project (Colombo et al. 2015). The start-ups have the additional opportunity to communicate new information through updates to their potential investors (Schramm and Carstens 2014).

Many campaigns apply the "first-come, first-served" principle. The start-up's stakes are distributed to the investors until the funding limit has been reached. The capital investors' pledge during the funding period is in most cases to participate in the funding if the campaign ultimately reaches its threshold. Because of this, the committed capital is kept in a trust or similar account until the end of the funding period. Reaching the threshold however does not signal the end of the campaign; overfunding up to a certain maximum funding limit is in fact possible. And success is still possible even if a campaign does not reach its targeted threshold. Some platforms decide to prolong the funding period in certain cases (Hornuf and Schwienbacher 2016; Hornuf and Neuenkirch 2015), and depending on the system, investors usually receive their money back in the case of a negative outcome. A negative funding outcome occurs if the amount of the collected money is below the funding threshold at the end of the funding period. The subscription phase is reached in the case of a positive outcome of the funding phase. When this is the case, the start-up company legally receives its funding and the investors obtain their shares. The sixth phase comprises the holding period of the stake, with the investor usually being obliged to hold the shares for a certain time period, which can be extended. The start-up here builds its business, regularly informing and updating its investors about the company's performance (Beck 2017). In the final exit stage phase, the investors sell their shares or alternatively give them back to the start-up (Hagedorn and Pinkwart 2013; Beck 2017).

3.2 *Fundraisers*

3.2.1 Entrepreneur Motivation

The typical equity crowdfunding fundraisers are entrepreneurs with start-up companies (Hornuf and Schwienbacher 2014b). The motivation of the entrepreneurs to engage in crowdinvesting as fundraisers is primarily financial, ultimately making crowdfunding a financing decision. Fundraisers use crowdfunding to efficiently collect capital. The decision is based on the equity crowdfunding's lower costs of capital. This is due to the intermediate function of the platform as it matches start-ups with investors who have a high willingness to provide capital to a start-up on a global level (Belleflamme et al. 2013, 2014).

Academic literature has identified other reasons for firms to participate in crowdinvesting. One factor is the access to additional information, especially feedbacks and support from investors. However, Agrawal et al. (2013) doubt that investor feedback has an informative value for the wider market. Certain companies expect support from their community network creation. The idea behind this is that the crowd not only has an interest in backing the young company financially but also with other own resources to increase the company's profits and investor returns as a result. This can be a knowledge-based support or customer advertisement of their product through the investors (Sannajust et al. 2014). Burtch et al. (2013) have shown that crowdfunding raises awareness for the venture and hence has a positive marketing effect. Fundraisers could also leverage crowdfunding to advertise their product directly to investors. Assuming that customers and investors match to a certain degree, companies can increase their understanding of their customers by learning from their investors. Moreover, entrepreneurs might want to use the campaign as a success validation of their idea by the investors through a positive funding campaign. Here, strong support for the campaign indicates that a large amount of people believe in the business idea (Belleflamme et al. 2014). However, while some of these factors have been scientifically validated, others remain scholarly assumptions and have yet to be confirmed. A recent survey of entrepreneurs engaging in donation, reward, and equity crowdfunding shows that the entrepreneurs use the campaigns to draw attention to and receive feedback for their project(s). The authors discovered that "getting public attention was relevant (or highly relevant) for over 85%, and obtaining feedback for the product/service offered was relevant (or highly relevant) for about 60% of the respondents" (Belleflamme et al. 2013, p. 322).

While there are compelling reasons for some entrepreneurs to choose equity crowdfunding as a source of capital collection, others tend to dismiss this option. Gleasure (2015) has identified three main reasons why entrepreneurs avoid crowdfunding as a financing tool: the fear of visible failure, the fear of projecting desperation, and the fear of disclosure. The fear of visible failure influences entrepreneurs who avoid crowdfunding because they think that the potential public failure of their crowdfunding campaign could have negative implications for finding future investors for their companies. Entrepreneurs often do not want to publish business model relevant or sensitive information, especially if they want to keep their first mover advantage. This tendency is especially seen in the business-to-customer (B2C) environment and to a lesser degree in the business-to-business (B2B) market. Fear of projecting desperation is the concern of entrepreneurs for whom "the mere act of adopting crowdfunding could create a negative external perception" (Gleasure 2015, p. 226).

3.2.2 Start-Up Funding

The entrepreneur's equity crowdfunding decision is generally arrived at in the general start-up funding context. Notably, it is often not the only funding source for the entrepreneurs (Agrawal et al. 2013). A German start-up requires on average €14,800 in capital for its establishment (Metzger 2015). Apart from their personal funds, many start-ups receive additional funding from family and friends, banks, public loans, government programs, business angel investors, and venture capitalists (Agrawal et al. 2013; Hagedorn and Pinkwart 2013; Belleflamme et al. 2013). Business angel investors as well as friends and family are most closely related to crowdinvesting. Angel investors provide start-ups with capital in early stages, also frequently offering specific industry knowledge and connections to support the venture (Beck 2017; Dorff 2013).

The funders' support to the start-up is influenced by the maturity of the firm. Understanding the main stages of the company's development and the financial support received during these phases in detail is relevant for entrepreneurs to select their funding appropriately. According to Schefczyk (2000), the development of a company is separated into three main stages: the *early stage* comprises the time preparing the company for its foundation. The *pre-establishment time* is sometimes separately described as the *seed stage*, which includes the creation of a business idea and the preparation of the business. The early stage also describes the period of the start-up's foundation and the establishment process of the business (Beck 2017). It has reached the expansion stage if the company initiates market penetration and expansion into new markets. The last stage is the late or maturity stage. Here, the company and investors prepare for the release of the company. At this point, an initial public offering is possible as an alternative. Finally, the "old" shareholders buy themselves out of the company (Schefczyk 2000).

Start-ups engaging in crowdinvesting are usually in the early stage (Hornuf and Schwienbacher 2014b) and experience a low availability of funding for their young companies. After this point however, the funding environment develops positively for the start-ups as the business matures. Entrepreneurs can thus select from a greater variety of funding sources in the expansion stage and the late stage. Late-stage funding is primarily conducted by venture capitalists, private equity, credits, stock markets, and strategic investors. Capital in the late stage in particular is extensively available for companies (Beck 2017). By contrast, in the early stage, the major financial support is provided by own funds together with financial backings from "friends, family and fools" (Kortleben and Vollmar 2012). Limited support from public funds as well as banks and even more limited backing by venture capitals and business angel investors are also obtainable for start-ups in the early stage. Start-ups in general encounter significant competition when it comes to collecting money for their companies. Public funding is often accompanied by high levels of bureaucracy and is consequently a complicated and time-intensive process. Financial institutes demand collateral for their financial support, and start-ups often do not possess the required amount of assets to obtain funding from banks (Cosh et al. 2009; Beck 2017). Business angel investors and venture capitalists are rare and provide only very selective funding. Out of the thousands of start-ups that manage to pique the interest of angel investors, only about 3% actually receive funding (Pope 2010). The European business angel investing market is furthermore relatively small compared to the USA (Hornuf and Schwienbacher 2014b), and the situation for venture capital funding is about the same. Between 1% and 5% of start-ups survive the venture capital's selection process and benefit from venture capital funding (Kortleben and Vollmar 2012). All in all, there is a notably higher demand for funding than the funding actually supplied by investors or financial and public institutions.

3.2.3 Early-Stage Gap and Substitution of Traditional Funding Sources

The money missing to fund all potential start-ups leads to the so-called early-stage gap (Hemer 2011). The lack of financial support resulting from the early-stage gap is a major motivation for start-ups to engage in equity crowdfunding (Hornuf and Schwienbacher 2014a). There are three main reasons for the early-stage gap. First is demand. Funders tend to unsystematically look for funding sources. Additionally, they might lack the right presentation skills to "pitch" their idea, and their potentially good business idea might therefore receive no funding (Beck 2017). Second, there is the investor side. According to Klöhn and Hornuf (2012, p. 257), professional institutional investors are generally not more successful in investing compared to the crowdinvestors who are usually nonprofessional investors. Professional investors potentially fund investments that might bring them, but not their clients, the highest profits (Beck 2017). Professional investors are also a homogenous group with a similar educational background and the same behavioral patterns (Klöhn and Hornuf 2012). Third, Germany has a relatively small venture capital market, and start-up investments are risk-laden (Hagedorn and Pinkwart 2013). Belleflamme et al. (2015) note that equity crowdfunding is especially attractive for entrepreneurs who have insufficient funds to establish or develop their start-up and cannot (or only under unfavorable conditions) obtain funds from traditional financial sources. Crowdinvesting therefore enables small entrepreneurs to receive funding from the general public (Hornuf and Neuenkirch 2015). The early-stage gap is thereby reduced due to the financial support from equity crowdfunding campaigns (Hemer 2011).

Crowdinvesting, as a relatively new funding option for start-ups, is (at least to a certain degree) likely to substitute other financial alternatives in the future. Hornuf and Schwienbacher (2014b) argue that for certain entrepreneurs, it is economically interesting to fund their start-ups with equity crowdfunding instead of with traditional funding sources. For instance, in the biotechnological start-up sector, crowdfunding is considered to be a future funding alternative. This is evidenced by the launch of several biotech-focused platforms in the USA (Bains et al. 2014). Some authors hold the opinion that crowdfunding competes directly with traditional investment sources. Burtch et al. (2013) show that crowdfunding participation drops when real estate prices are higher, whereas the capital in crowdinvesting increases amidst more volatile stock markets (Hornuf and Neuenkirch 2015). Blaseg and Koetter (2015) discovered that German start-ups use equity crowdfunding notably more often if their bank is in an economically unfavorable situation. Crowdinvesting and the related angel investing partially substitute for one another due to their similar investment. Still, both funding sources complement each other in many other cases, especially in the case of co-investments (Hornuf and Schwienbacher 2016).

3.3 *Investors*

3.3.1 Motivation and Characteristics of the Investors

The main motivation for investors is a financial return on their investment (Agrawal et al. 2013). Beck (2017) assumes that crowdinvesting potentially has an additional nonfinancial psychological effect for investors who want to support a project because of its positive appearance as well as the pioneer thinking of the start-up. In theory, this could be the case. Academic studies in donation- and reward-based crowdfunding have demonstrated that backers' financial contributions are motivated by the rewards, by the positive feeling of supporting a project, and by having the opportunity to engage in a creative community (Gerber et al. 2012). Brem and Wassong (2014) however have found to the contrary that emotional and supportive reasons do not play a relevant role for an investor's crowdinvesting decision. This is in line with the findings of Cholakova and Clarysse (2015) who discovered that nonfinancial motivations generally have no effect on pledging behavior and that only financial aspects motivate investors to engage in equity crowdfunding. The capital return of crowdinvesting is a key difference to reward-based crowdfunding. Reward backers only receive a specified reward and are not able to benefit from the future performance of the company. This can be especially frustrating for backers if the product or company is later acquired by venture capitalists or a company. One prominent example is the acquisition of *Oculus Rift* by *Facebook* after the virtual reality headset had received large support in a reward-based crowdfunding campaign.

Investors are able to engage in equity crowdfunding with small capital contributions. Consequently, it requires a large quantity of investors to collect the required amount of money (Beck 2017). A large number of participants have in the past led to high transaction costs for communication and the collection of money. The risks here basically have the potential to make crowdfunding an insufficient funding method (Bradford 2012). However, the corresponding transaction costs are significantly reduced with the help of the Internet (Hornuf and Schwienbacher 2014b). Crowdfunding these days benefits from an efficient matching of fundraisers and backers, making communication costs lower, which facilitates backer participation in a project, the monitoring of the venture, and information collection (Agrawal et al. 2013).

Playing a curtailing role in the success of start-up funding, the typical crowdfunding investor can be described with the following specific characteristics. The funding conditions of equity crowdfunding are comparable to donation- or reward-based crowdfunding, which is often used for creative projects, even though start-up investors generally differ from the creative industry's supporters (Hemer 2011). In the general crowdfunding environment, one out of two Germans have heard of the term crowdfunding, and about 25% of the total population knows what the term means. The typical German providing capital to one of the crowdfunding types is male, between 18 and 38 years old, has a college degree, and is in a higher income bracket. Seven percent of Germans have provided money to a crowdfunding campaign (Harms 2015).

Specifically speaking, the typical profile of a crowdinvestor is risk-taking and a user of the Internet and financial online transactions. The investor aims to invest his capital to achieve a profit by evaluating crowdfunding business ideas (Beck 2017). The typical crowdinvestor is 39 years old and works in fields often related to the financial or innovation industry. Further, he or she is experienced in the capital market. Although a number of crowdinvestors are also professional venture capitalists, equity crowdfunding investors are in general nonprofessional investors (Klöhn and Hornuf 2012; Beck 2017). Crowdinvestors are gradually replacing specialized financial investors who work for banks, for venture capital companies, or as business angel investors when it comes to funding start-ups (Belleflamme et al. 2014). Agrawal et al. (2011) point out that the average crowdinvestor differs noticeably from the traditional investor in geographic terms. The majority of business angel investors live in metropolitan areas, conducting their investments in start-ups close to where they are living. Consequently, certain start-ups are geographically discriminated against and excluded from this funding opportunity (Gelfond and Foti 2012; Sohl 1999). Venture capitalists also typically concentrate their investments on a regional level. Crowdfunding bypasses these geographic restrictions with the support of online communication, with local crowdinvestors participating early on and with larger amounts in a campaign (Agrawal et al. 2011).

3.3.2 Profit Sharing and Accretion of Start-Ups

The major reason for crowdinvestors to participate in equity crowdfunding is the financial benefit they receive from their investment. Therefore, the design of the investor's stake is a crucial point of crowdinvesting and is especially important when attracting investors (Cholakova and Clarysse 2015; Brem and Wassong 2014). Crowdinvesting is based on the idea of performance-sharing (Schramm and Carstens 2014), which is split into profit sharing and accretion. Profit sharing is the partial sharing of the start-up's annual profit with the investor. Accretion is based on the start-up's valuation at the beginning and end of the investment. Typically, the investor receives an under-proportional stake in the company because the funders bear a notably higher risk (Beck 2017).

However, investors demand profitable investments, so two contradicting interests have to be considered when evaluating the start-up (Brem and Wassong 2014). Due to information asymmetry between the start-up and the investors, investors have only limited possibilities to conduct their own evaluation of the company. They have to trust the start-up's and the platform's assessment because of their lack of accessibility to value-relevant information (Sannajust et al. 2014). Also, the investments are on average small, making a complex assessment uneconomical (Dorff 2013). On the one hand, the start-up becomes unattractive for the investors if it is evaluated too high at the beginning of the investment. This leads to smaller percentage stakes of the start-up for the investors, who consequently receive a lower profit sharing. Additionally, they do not benefit from accretion as optimally as they could. The revaluation of the company at the exit stage would lead to a lower accretion because the company was already unreasonably highly valued at the beginning of the investment. On the other hand, entrepreneurs have an interest in valuing their start-up at a high level at the beginning of the investment and low at the exit stage of the investment period. This is driven by the intent to keep as much control of the company and money for themselves as possible. Overall, finding the right balance between funder and investor interests for the start-up evaluation is a key challenge of equity crowdfunding (Beck 2017).

3.3.3 Information Asymmetry and Profitability of Investments

One of the key differences between non-equity and equity crowdfunding is information asymmetries. In a donation and reward-based crowdfunding context, the importance for the backers is whether the funded campaign will be successful and if the product will be delivered. In a crowdinvesting context, information asymmetries have a higher importance because the evaluation has to assess whether the start-up will generate the expected returns or not (Agrawal et al. 2011). The investors undertake risk assessments which include the expected start-up performance in the future. Main concerns here include the ability of the start-up to attract enough customers to be profitable (Belleflamme et al. 2015). Altogether, the early stage of ventures intensifies the information asymmetry because it is only partially regulated, and past information on start-ups generally does not exist (Agrawal et al. 2013).

However, even if investors decide to invest in crowdinvesting campaigns despite large information asymmetries, it is not clear whether these investments are financially rewarding. Although there is (limited) information available on the success and return rates of equity crowdfunding investments, scholars disagree about the profitability of crowdfunding investments. Agrawal et al. (2013) point out that promising high-quality start-ups have other, more attractive options to obtain funding. In line with this, Dorff (2013) argues that entrepreneurs avoid equity crowdfunding and tend to select other funding sources such as business angels if they have the possibility to do so. Funding types such as angel investing are connected to nonmonetary benefits for the start-up, including the angel's experience and advice. The remaining start-ups engaging in crowdinvesting therefore have a relatively high failure rate. Hence, the majority of the investments will fail and generate negative returns. The author concludes that the risk is too high given the potential returns. Beck (2017) opposes Dorff's (2013) view that equity crowdfunding is on the whole unattractive for start-ups. Funding sources such as venture capitalists often demand a high stake or a large share in the company or have other demands toward the start-up. This can be a reason for promising start-ups to select equity crowdfunding. Further, the number of start-ups which don't receive funding from business angel investors is quite large (although this does not automatically indicate low business quality) (Pope 2010). Many start-ups also do not have the size for the angel investment or venture capital market and thus require funding from other sources (Hornuf and Schwienbacher 2014a). All in all, crowd investments are high risk. Their attractiveness as an investment type depends for investors on the extent of the profit-sharing and accretion agreement. The number of start-up failures is also a factor.

3.4 Platforms

3.4.1 Function of Platforms

Equity crowdfunding platforms are used as intermediates for the funding of start-ups (Lambert and Schwienbacher 2010). Their design promotes the presentation of the fundraiser's project and the business plan to the crowd and is therefore a suitable application for early-stage entrepreneurs (Agrawal et al. 2011). Matching and managing the interaction of the two markets sides, it is described as a two-sided platform market. The service provided is a one-to-many, i.e., a start-up to crowd pairing (Belleflamme et al. 2015). Platforms are also used for follow-up funding, although the option to initiate a second funding round has to date been sparsely used by entrepreneurs (Hornuf and Schwienbacher 2014a). Klöhn and Hornuf (2012) indicate that the platforms have a selective process to identify appropriate and promising start-up ideas. For instance, out of 40 applications, only one start-up is ultimately financed on the German platform *Seedmatch*. The reason for this is the double assessment process for start-ups. First, the crowdinvesting platform "fulfills a screening and coordination function of the possible investments" (Hagedorn and Pinkwart 2013, p. 21). After this preselection, only the start-ups chosen by the platform are presented on its webpage. The crowd then filters the published projects. Second, another selection takes place because the projects only get funded if they have reached the threshold at the end of the funding period (Beck 2017).

Crowdfunding can also be initiated without the platform as the intermediate. Start-ups initiate direct equity fundraising when funds are collected over a special company webpage. Nonetheless, start-ups generally use the indirect funding model (Lambert and Schwienbacher 2010). Platforms offer a standardized process of capital collection, while the direct individual crowdfunding initiatives are more flexible when adapting to a start-up's needs. The direct approach has the advantage that funders are able to offer a large variety of financial and nonfinancial compensations to the investors. However, the amount of capital collected through direct crowdfunding is smaller compared to platform funding (Belleflamme et al. 2014). Gleasure (2015) notes that the numbers of direct crowdfunding campaigns have increased in recent years.

3.4.2 Platform Design

Crowdinvesting platforms differ in their design. Hornuf and Schwienbacher (2014a) explain this heterogeneity as being a result of the market's novelty, varying investor demands, different laws, and other market differentiations. These factors allow a certain space for the platforms to experiment with their business models. One of these dimensions is the type of securities which the start-ups offer to their investors. These can be equity type notes or company shares. The platforms determine the minimum investment required. This limitation can range from no required minimum participation amount up to several thousand euros, with the platforms either focusing solely on equity crowdfunding or the crowdinvesting service being offered in combination with other crowdfunding types such as donation- or reward-based crowdfunding (Beck 2017). They also set the rules regarding whether the investor is investing "directly in the startup or pooled through a special purpose vehicle" (Hornuf and Schwienbacher 2014a, p. 2). Platforms impose minimum funding levels to regulate which kind of investor participates in the funding. No restrictions at all allow every investor to engage in the campaign, while other platforms set high capital requirements in an attempt to target wealthy investors. Another aspect is the platform's commission. Generally, they collect no money from the investor, but from the fundraisers instead, with the platforms receiving fees or commissions raging in Germany from 5% to 10% of the money collected during a campaign (Hornuf and Schwienbacher 2014a; Beck 2017).

3.4.3 All-or-Nothing and Keep-It-All Model

Two alternative capital collection models offered by crowdfunding platforms are the *all-or-nothing* and the *keep-it-all* models (Cumming et al. 2020). The most-applied model of the all-or-nothing principle regulates that the funding threshold has to be reached within the pledging period to obtain the capital (Mollick 2014). The keep-it-all model is a threshold-independent approach which is occasionally used for crowdinvesting. Funds for the project are provided immediately to start-ups, and the entrepreneurs can keep them even if the threshold has not been reached (Martínez-Cañas et al. 2012). All-or-nothing crowdfunding projects have notably larger funding goals compared to the keep-it-all model. On the one hand, the latter is more successful for smaller, general crowdfunding projects. On the other hand, the all-or-nothing model is a guarantee to the investors that start-ups will not initiate an unrealistic, low funding goal. If the start-up has reached the funding threshold, it has adequate capital to establish the start-up idea and will not be under financial pressure because of its insufficient funds (Cumming et al. 2020). All-or-nothing campaigns are successful 44% of the time (Freedman and Nutting 2015). This is less than the average success rate of German crowdfunding campaigns, which is about 60% (Für-Gründer.de 2015). Furthermore, all German equity crowdfunding portals apply the all-or-nothing model (Hornuf and Schwienbacher 2015).

3.5 Benefits and Risks

3.5.1 Benefits

Like every financial investment, equity crowdfunding is accompanied by certain benefits and risks. Its benefits were discussed above: crowdinvesting can reduce the early-stage funding gap for young companies (Beck 2017) and is, therefore, an appealing funding alternative for start-ups when compared to traditional funding sources such as banks and venture capitalists. It is an opportunity to attract further investors (Schramm and Carstens 2014). Entrepreneurs can profit from funding without geographical investor restrictions (Agrawal et al. 2011). Crowdinvestors benefit from access to a large number of start-ups. They can use the opportunity to invest in a range of dynamic and attractive entrepreneurial ideas (Beck 2017), with capital generating profit through financial returns (Cholakova and Claryssc 2015). Another compelling aspect is flexibility. Entrepreneurs can benefit from the "flexibility regarding the length of the financing period, the frequency of the recourse and the amount of money" (Hagedorn and Pinkwart 2013, p. 5). Platforms facilitate the matching of both the investor and fundraiser sides. Equity crowdfunding is additionally an uncomplicated system with low bureaucratic obstacles. The investor's as well as start-up's sides profit from easy-to-handle processes. Funding can be conducted with a low amount of individual capital costs. The overall sums collected for the start-up are large due to the multiplying effect of the crowd investments. Entrepreneurs can use their successful funding to promote their creditworthiness, which results in easier access to venture capital or bank funding. Also, if a lot of investors invest capital within a short period of time in a certain project, it is an indicator of the marketability of the project idea. The marketing effect of a project campaign can be an additional benefit of equity crowdfunding (Belleflamme et al. 2015; Beck 2017).

3.5.2 Fundraisers' Risks

Equity crowdfunding also bears risks for fundraisers and investors. Entrepreneurs face a certain risk associated with crowdinvesting. First, the preparation of the campaign requires time, and success is not guaranteed (Schramm and Carstens 2014). Second, a negative outcome of a campaign could ultimately decrease the chances of finding future investors for a project (Gleasure 2015). Third, companies face a major increase in the number of stakeholders with crowdfunding. This can influence the corporate structure, bringing potential strategic and legal consequences for the company. Examples here include tax issues or the choice of entity (Gelfond and Foti 2012). Fourth, the disclosure requirement for the company bears certain risk for entrepreneurs. If the venture is publishing sensitive information, other competitors might also become informed and imitate the product or business plan. Fifth, entrepreneurs potentially do not profit from their investors in the holding period because of their lower experience compared to professional investors. Moreover, a large number of investors supporting the project could overwhelm small ventures (Agrawal et al. 2013).

3.5.3 Investors' Risks

The first risk for a crowdfunding investor arises from potential failures among the funded projects. Investments in the early stage of companies are inherently risky (Agrawal et al. 2013). This can lead to the bankruptcy of companies and capital losses for investors (European Securities and Markets Authority 2014). Heckmann and Schnabel (2005) estimate that in general only one-third of start-ups in Germany will survive the first 6 years of their existence. Beck (2017) assumes for equity crowdfunding start-ups that the bankruptcy rate will remain in the lower range of 15% and 20% because of the platforms' and investors' preselection process and the high starting capital coming from funding. However, the complete loss of a specific investment has to be examined in light of the overall picture. The invested amounts of money are usually low, and investors generally diversify their risk by investing in several start-ups. Second, the selection process of platforms can be also risky, being potentially one-sided because employees are mainly young people with a tendency toward online business models. Thus, classic business models with a real-life context might have a lower chance of acceptance. The third risk originates in the course of the low investments. The low sums lead to a low investor incentive to conduct sufficient due diligence. The control of specific details of the equity crowdfunding process such as contracts and provided financial information is not necessarily reasonable and economic for the investor (Wilson and Testoni 2014). Further, investors could potentially overestimate the due diligence conducted by the platforms. Fourth, there is the risk of an exaggerated start-up valuation, which has an impact on future profits. This could ultimately lead to low returns of investments in the future because investors only hold a small stake in the company. Also, the liquidation of investments is limited because of the long-term orientation of the investment (European Securities and Markets Authority 2014; Beck 2017).

There is also the *dilution* risk associated with equity crowdfunding. This describes the situation where a company provides new shares of its entity to new investors, which affects previous investors because "each share (including those previously issued) represents a smaller percentage of the company" (Dorff 2013, p. 516). Dilution can have a positive as well as negative effect on previous investors, depending whether the new investors have paid more or less for the shares than the company is actually worth. Crowdfunding investors can lose major stakes here in the case of a negative outcome. Platforms can avoid this situation by setting up a contract limiting or restricting the dilution right(s) of the fundraisers.

Information asymmetry between a start-up and investors is another risk factor. The nonprofessional average investor might not have access to value-relevant information (Sannajust et al. 2014). This is increased by the fact that the fundraiser's company is generally relatively new (Hornuf and Schwienbacher 2014a). Hence there is almost no past performance information available, making investment decisions even riskier. Another critical aspect is that investors are not directly able to control how the companies who initiate the funding use the collected capital. The lack of appropriate monitor measurements can result in start-up behavior contrary to an investor's interests (Belleflamme et al. 2015; Wilson and Testoni 2014). Investors also have to face the risk of fraud. There is the potential risk of imposters using false information to collect investor money, although the assessment and preselection of the projects through the crowdinvesting platforms notably reduces this risk (Agrawal et al. 2013). So far, not a single case of equity crowdfunding fraud has been reported (Dresner 2014). There are also risks emerging out of the investor-platform relationship. There could be conflicts of interest for the platform because of potential stakes in start-ups. Also, a platform failure could have severe consequences for the investors in cases where platforms administrate investors' assets (European Securities and Markets Authority 2014). Some authors raise the negative argument that crowdinvesting is altogether a too-risky investment because only start-ups which are rejected by venture capitals and others decide to engage in equity crowdfunding (Agrawal et al. 2013; Dorff 2013). However, according to Beck, this is unfounded because venture capitalists normally invest in later stages. Also, start-ups might prefer crowdinvesting to venture capitalists (Beck 2017). All in all, the interaction of investors, fundraisers, and platforms in the equity crowdfunding process has several potential risks. Some can be influenced by the actors, while others are system risks.

4 Crowdfunding Markets in Liechtenstein, Austria, Germany, and Switzerland

The markets for crowdfunding in the four German-speaking countries differ in their development and size. While Germany and Switzerland are already well-developed, the average spending on crowdfunding projects in Austria remains low. Liechtenstein has only one platform for donation-based crowdfunding, but no own platform for crowdlending or crowdinvesting.

4.1 German Campaigns

Today, the German crowdinvesting market serves as an additional option for start-ups to collect capital for their venture. So far, five academic studies have analyzed the German equity crowdfunding market. Hornuf and Schwienbacher (2014a, 2015) conducted two large studies in 2013 and 2014, where they were able to identify distinctive patterns of the German market. Receiving data from all 15 major crowdfunding platforms (mentioned earlier), they collected in their first study a sample of 168 successful and unsuccessful German campaigns that lasted until the end of 2013, as well as an additional 244 cases from other European countries (Hornuf and Schwienbacher 2014a). The authors subsequently carried out a second study with the four largest German platforms: *Innovestment*, *Companisto*, *Seedmatch*, and *United Equity*. This study is comprised of 88 campaigns with a total of 26,967 single investment decisions (Hornuf and Schwienbacher 2015). Another study conducted by Blaseg and Koetter (2015) collected a sample of 157 campaigns from *Bankless24*, *Bergfuerst*, *Companisto*, *Fundsters*, *Innovestment*, *Mashup Finance*, and *Seedmatch* lasting to mid-2014. Finally, Biering et al. (2014) used data from *Seedmatch* and *Companisto* as well as expert interviews to present the German crowdinvesting environment.

The German companies conducting campaigns are on average 1.84 years old. This is a relatively young enterprise age and suits the academic findings that crowdinvesting ventures are usually in their early stages (Hornuf and Schwienbacher 2014b). German start-ups engaging in equity crowdfunding tend to be riskier than start-ups using traditional bank financing. The crowdfunding start-ups have fewer tangible assets and are smaller than their non-crowdinvesting counterparts, having a higher information asymmetry. The type of management team has no influence on whether a start-up applies equity crowdfunding or not (Blaseg and Koetter 2015). German crowdinvestors tend to focus, according to Biering et al. (2014), on projects which already have a product and revenues. Investments in earlier stage start-ups are relatively rare and predominantly observed in the high-tech sector.

The campaign duration is on average 45.75 days. The typical start-up was established as a limited liability company (the German *GmbH*) (Hornuf and Schwienbacher 2015). The required minimum investment amount is generally low. Only 26.9% of the campaigns required investments of €250 or more, while the platforms demanded an average fee of 8% of the funding. The German-specific type of security "participation loan" (*partiarische Darlehen*) was used by 29% of the start-ups to enable investor participation (Hornuf and Schwienbacher 2014a). The start-ups received on an average campaign day seven investments of an average €660 per investment. Only 3% of the investments were above €5000, which indicates that large investments are rather unusual. The platforms had on average six active campaigns on each crowdinvesting website. 15.7% of the German campaigns did not reach their threshold and were unsuccessful as a result (Hornuf and Schwienbacher 2014a, 2015). This is in line with the calculated success rate of 85% by Blaseg and Koetter (2015). Three campaigns had each reached three million euros in pledges by mid-2014. Also, a low number of start-ups initiated a follow-up funding; these cases are expected to increase (Hornuf and Schwienbacher 2014a). On average, 280 investors funded €200,000 per project, and the ventures were valued at €1.95 million. Therefore, after the funding period, approximately 10% of the start-ups' share was crowdinvestor-owned (Blaseg and Koetter 2015). Hornuf and Schwienbacher (2014a) identified in their study an average of 215 investors per campaign. Notably, the targeted thresholds were on average at €72,057, while the actual collected capital was about €154,000. Hence, the German entrepreneurs collected on average double the amount of capital that they were targeting with their threshold. The differentiating numbers provided by Blaseg and Koetter (2015) and Hornuf and Schwienbacher (2014a) can be explained by the dissimilar sampling of the campaigns in a different time frame. The collected capital per campaign was, for instance, €354,000 in 2015, while it was €264,000 in 2014 (Für-Gründer.de 2015). The German ventures on average raised less capital per campaign compared to other European countries (Hornuf and Schwienbacher 2014a).

4.2 German Investors

German investors support a high number of start-ups from the information-technology sector in German crowdinvesting campaigns (Hagedorn and Pinkwart 2013), contributing €489.13 on average. Seedmatching investors expect on average a 25% yearly return on their crowdfunding investment, with 70% of them expecting a return between 1% and 20% (Biering et al. 2014). German investors can be separated into several groups based on their investment behaviors: fun investors, family and friends' investors, product fans, revenue investors, and "crowd angels." The fun investors contribute small amounts and see it as an interesting and enjoyable experience. As relatives of the entrepreneurs, the family and friends' investors support them with larger pledges and tend to promote the campaign. The product fans are not return focused and instead select a specific campaign because they are attracted to the product. An incentive is the product's preemption. The return is primarily the focus of the quality signal-oriented revenue investors. This type invests €250 or more and conducts a relatively large assessment of the start-ups. They are also influenced by the pledges of other investors and customer reports. The last German investor profile is the "crowd angel" with intensive venture assessments and investments of usually €5000 or more. This person invests in fewer start-ups compared to the revenue investors but supports the entrepreneurs on a high level (Biering et al. 2014). In summary, the German start-ups have been using equity crowdfunding for a couple of years, with several German platforms offering their service to them. Most of the campaigns are successful with an average collected capital of several hundred thousand euros and 200 to 300 investors with different characteristics (Biering et al. 2014; Blaseg and Koetter 2015; Hagedorn and Pinkwart 2013; Hornuf and Schwienbacher 2014a).

5 An Outlook at Cross-Border Crowdfunding

Although crowdfunding campaigns are theoretically easy to establish over the Internet, there are three main obstacles that currently limit the success of cross-border crowdfunding: behavioral biases of potential investors, e.g., the home bias or differing social attitudes, multiple tax systems, and multiple legislation. These factors are very important for crowdfunding projects and platforms that are in need of cross-border financing. Projects with their origin in small countries such as Liechtenstein constantly face the limitation of potential financing within a country with only a few people and therefore have only minor investment potential. Although of major importance, little or no research has been conducted that examines these factors. We will be working to fill this gap in the near future.

5.1 Behavioral Biases

Home bias is the tendency of investors to invest in companies and ideas that are geographically close to them, often under the misconception of knowing these companies and their business opportunities better than others. Lin and Viswanathan (2016) point out that home bias is still a robust phenomenon in investing, even in the field of crowdfunding. It is difficult to convince these kinds of investors to also invest abroad. Another important behavioral factor is the role of globally differing social attitudes and emotional differences. It is important for the success of a crowdfunding project to run a marketing and positioning campaign of the product that suits potential investors. In other words, potential German and potential Swiss investors must be mobilized differently when attempting to "grab their attention" with a specific project.

5.2 Multiple Tax Systems

Crowdfunding investors have to pay taxes when investing and earning in a crowdfunding project. Taxation depends on the combination of countries involved (residence of the investor, platform, and project), the type of crowdfunding (lending or equity-based), and potential tax exemptions and legal expenses. If, for example, a German resident invests in an Austrian equity crowdfunding project, his interest payments as well as any bonuses have to be taxed under the German progressive income tax law, and additional legal costs (*Zessionsgebühr*) might apply. If this same investor invests in a German project, he would have to pay 25% capital gains tax plus a 5.5% solidarity surcharge (this tax is automatically paid by the project company). This simple example from two similar neighboring countries reveals that taxation can vary greatly when taking cross-border differences into account.

5.3 Multiple Legislation

Legislators have a major influence on the specific equity crowdfunding market of each country. This funding used to be restricted in the USA and still is in other countries (Ahlers et al. 2015). The main driver for governments to create crowdinvesting laws is the protection of the investors. While an increase in crowdfunding regulations supports investor protections, it has downsides for the overall equity crowdfunding market. Hornuf and Schwienbacher (2014b) point out that "more investor protection leads to fewer crowdinvesting campaigns" (p. 25). The authors argue that in the worst case, the start-up is not able to obtain funding via crowdinvesting. Consequently, new laws potentially reduce the number of the entrepreneurial ventures (Hornuf and Schwienbacher 2014b). European countries have in comparison implemented lower legal obstacles for equity crowdfunding and have hence experienced a development in the crowdinvesting market (Hornuf and Schwienbacher 2014b). Generally, there is no prospectus requirement for European start-ups initiating crowdfunding campaigns of less than €100,000 per year. Individual European Union member states can have higher limits or specific rules allowing exemptions with a certain number or type of investor. European legislators have become aware of the potential of equity crowdfunding in recent years, and several countries have adapted and/or will adapt their laws to make them more suitable for crowdinvesting (Hornuf and Schwienbacher 2014b). The European Securities and Markets Authority (2014) states that the majority of European platforms have structured their business models in a way to bypass certain European and national legal requirements. Hornuf and Schwienbacher (2014b) furthermore point out that entrepreneurs do this to avoid related compliance costs.

6 Conclusion

Crowdfunding and equity crowdfunding/crowdinvesting in particular are relatively new phenomena that are based on older trends and are fostered by Internet usage (Hagedorn and Pinkwart 2013; Hemer 2011; Lawton et al. 2012). Connecting companies and investors with the support of platforms to collect capital for young companies, equity crowdfunding has the ability to reduce the early-stage gap of company funding (Hornuf and Schwienbacher 2014b; Ordanini et al. 2011). Compared to its related financial collection schemes, donation-, reward-, and lending-based crowdfunding is a relatively complex type of funding (Wilson and Testoni 2014; Bradford 2012). A typical crowdinvesting process begins with the application of the start-up, continues with the funding of the selected start-up, and ends after the holding phase with the exit of the investor (Hagedorn and Pinkwart 2013). Investments in crowdinvesting campaigns are simultaneously connected to high risk and opportunity (Cholakova and Clarysse 2015; Dorff 2013). Entrepreneurs select crowdinvesting because they primarily want to collect capital (Belleflamme et al. 2013), and platforms are the intermediates between the company and its investors (Lambert and Schwienbacher 2010). They also conduct a preselection of the companies' applications (Hagedorn and Pinkwart 2013). The all-or-nothing model is the most commonly applied model when a funding threshold has to be reached within the pledging period to obtain the capital (Cumming et al. 2020; Hornuf and Schwienbacher 2015). One of the crucial points of crowdinvesting is the evaluation, which directly influences the financial outcome for the investor (Beck 2017). Thanks to its liberal legislation, Germany is one of the catalysts of crowdinvesting (Klöhn et al. 2016). Overall, equity crowdfunding is poised to establish itself as a viable financing alternative for young companies (Für-Gründer.de 2015; Schramm and Carstens 2014), raising the question of how start-ups can use equity crowdfunding in the most effective and efficient way.

The literature has identified other reasons apart from financial motivation for why entrepreneurs select crowdfunding. First, they use it because investors provide them with valuable feedback (Agrawal et al. 2013; Belleflamme et al. 2013). Second, they want to use it as a success validation. If a large number of investors fund a campaign, it is an indicator that a large amount of people believe in the potential of the business idea (Belleflamme et al. 2014). Third, they choose crowdinvesting because they expect to profit from the additional support of the investors through a network creation via crowdinvesting (Sannajust et al. 2014).

Although a solid amount of research on crowdfunding per se is available, cross-border issues remain neglected. Cross-border crowdfunding is especially important for small countries such as Liechtenstein, where investment potential is limited. Thus far, we have identified three key factors to consider when targeting cross-border investors: behavioral biases, multiple taxation system, and multiple legislation. Future research should build upon these initial results.

References

Agrawal A, Catalini C, Goldfarb A (2011) Friends, family, and the flat world: the geography of crowdfunding. NBER Working Paper, 16820
Agrawal A, Catalini C, Goldfarb A (2013) Some simple economics of crowdfunding. NBER Working Paper, 19133
Ahlers GK, Cumming D, Günther C, Schweizer D (2015) Signaling in equity crowdfunding. Entrep Theory Pract 39(4):955–980
Bains W, Wooder S, Guzman DRM (2014) Funding biotech start-ups in a post-VC world. J Commer Biotechnol 20(1):10–27
Beck R (2017) Crowdinvesting: Die Investition der Vielen. Börsenbuchverlag
Belleflamme P, Lambert T, Schwienbacher A (2013) Individual crowdfunding practices. Ventur Cap 15(4):313–333
Belleflamme P, Lambert T, Schwienbacher A (2014) Crowdfunding: tapping the right crowd. J Bus Ventur 29(5):585–609
Belleflamme P, Omrani N, Peitz M (2015) The economics of crowdfunding platforms. Inf Econ Policy 33:11–28
Biering B, Hölzner H, Kortleben H (2014) Zukunftsperspektiven im Crowdinvesting: Eine Analyse der Entwicklung in Deutschland zwischen 2011 und 2014. EFNW AN-Institut der Universität Oldenburg
Blaseg D, Koetter M (2015) Friend or foe? Crowdfunding versus credit when banks are stressed. IWH Discussion Papers, 8
Bouncken RB, Komorek M, Kraus S (2015) Crowdfunding: the current state of research. Int Bus Econ Res J 13(4):407–416
Bradford CS (2012) Crowdfunding and the federal securities laws. Columbia Bus Law Rev 2012:1–150
Brem A, Wassong N (2014) Wer investiert warum - Eine Analyse von Investmententscheidungen bei Crowdfunding-Projekten. ZfKE–Zeitschrift für KMU und Entrepreneurship 62(1):31–55
Burtch G, Ghose A, Wattal S (2013) An empirical examination of the antecedents and consequences of contribution patterns in crowd-funded markets. Inf Syst Res 24(3):499–519
Cholakova M, Clarysse B (2015) Does the possibility to make equity investments in crowdfunding projects crowd out reward–based investments? Entrep Theory Pract 39(1):145–172
Colombo MG, Franzoni C, Rossi-Lamastra C (2015) Internal social capital and the attraction of early contributions in crowdfunding. Entrep Theory Pract 39(1):75–100
Cosh A, Cumming D, Hughes A (2009) Outside enterpreneurial capital. Econ J 119:1494–1533
Crosetto P, Regner T (2014) Crowdfunding: determinants of success and funding dynamics. Jena Economic Research Papers, 2014 – 035
Cumming DJ, Leboeuf G, Schwienbacher A (2020) Crowdfunding models: keep-it-all vs. all-or-nothing. Financ Manag 49(2):331–360
Deffains-Crapsky C, Sudolska A (2014) Radical innovation and early stage financing gaps: equity-based crowdfunding challenges. J Posit Manag 5(2):3–19
Dorff MB (2013) The siren call of equity crowdfunding. J Corp Law 39(3):493–524
Dresner S (2014) Crowdfunding: A guide to raising capital on the internet. Wiley, Hoboken, NJ
European Securities and Markets Authority (2014) Advice: investment-based crowdfunding
Freedman DM, Nutting MR (2015) Equity crowdfunding for investors: a guide to risks, returns, regulations, funding portals, due diligence, and deal terms. Wiley, Hoboken, NJ
Für-Gründer.de (2015) Crowdfinanzierung in Deutschland. https://www.fuer-gruender.de/fileadmin/mediapool/Unsere_Studien/Crowdfinanzierung_9M_2015_Fuer-Gruender.de_Dentons.pdf
Gelfond SH, Foti AD (2012) US $500 and a click: investing the "crowdfunding" way. J Invest Compliance 13(4):9–13

Gerber EM, Hui JS, Kuo P-Y (2012) Crowdfunding: why people are motivated to post and fund projects on crowdfunding platforms. In: Proceedings of the international workshop on design, influence, and social technologies: techniques, impacts and ethics, 11
Gleasure R (2015) Resistance to crowdfunding among entrepreneurs: an impression management perspective. J Strateg Inf Syst 24(4):219–233
Hagedorn A, Pinkwart A (2013) Crowdinvesting as a financing instrument for startups in Germany: a critical platform analysis. HHL Working Paper, 120
Harms M (2015) Crowd-funding Umfrage Bekanntheit and Beteiligung. Crowdfunding.de, Berlin. https://www.crowdfunding.de/app/uploads/2019/04/Crowdfunding-Umfrage-April-2015.pdf
Heckmann M, Schnabel C (2005) Überleben und Beschäftigungsentwicklung neu gegründeter Betriebe. Discussion Papers, 39
Hemer J (2011) A snapshot on crowdfunding. Arbeitspapiere Unternehmen und Region, R2/2011
Hornuf L, Neuenkirch M (2015) Pricing the value of cash flow rights in crowdinvesting: an analysis of Innovestment backers. Research papers in economics, 7/15
Hornuf L, Schwienbacher A (2014a) The emergence of crowdinvesting in Europe. Munich Discussion Paper, 43
Hornuf L, Schwienbacher A (2014b) Should securities regulation promote crowdinvesting? Munich Discussion Paper, 27
Hornuf L, Schwienbacher A (2015) Funding dynamics in crowdinvesting. Beiträge zur Jahrestagung des Vereins für Socialpolitik 2015: Ökonomische Entwicklung - Theorie und Politik - Session: Financial Economics II No. B10-V3
Hornuf L, Schwienbacher A (2016) Crowdinvesting: angel investing for the masses? In: Mason C, Landstrom H (eds) Handbook of research on venture capital. Edward Elgar Publishing, Cheltenham, UK
Klöhn L, Hornuf L (2012) Crowdinvesting in Deutschland. Zeitschrift für Bankrecht und Bankwirtschaft 24(4):237–266
Klöhn L, Hornuf L, Schilling T (2016) The regulation of crowdfunding in the German small investor protection act: content, consequences, critique, suggestions. Eur Company Law 13(2):56–66
Kortleben H, Vollmar BH (2012) Crowdinvesting: Eine alternative in der Gründungsfinanzierung? PFH research papers, 2012/06
Kuppuswamy V, Bayus BL (2013) Crowdfunding creative ideas: the dynamics of projects backers in Kickstarter. SSRN Working Paper, 2234765
Lambert T, Schwienbacher A (2010) An empirical analysis of crowdfunding. Soc Sci Res Netw 1578175:1–23
Lawton K, Marom D, Lawton K (2012) Crowdfunding revolution: how to raise venture capital using social media. McGraw Hill, New York
Lin M, Viswanathan S (2016) Home bias in online investments: an empirical study of an online crowdfunding market. Manag Sci 62(5):1393–1414
Martínez-Cañas R, Ruiz-Palomino P, del Pozo-Rubio R (2012) Crowdfunding and social networks in the music industry: implications for entrepreneurship. Int Bus Econ Res J 11(13):1471–1476
Massolution C (2015) Crowdfunding industry report. http://reports.crowdsourcing.org/index.php
Metzger G (2015) KfW-Gründungsmonitor 2015: Gründungstätigkeit nimmt zu–freiberufliche Tätigkeitsfelder dominieren. KfW Bankengruppe, Frankfurt
Mollick E (2014) The dynamics of crowdfunding: an exploratory study. J Bus Ventur 29(1):1–16
Moritz A, Block JH (2014) Crowdfunding und Crowdinvesting: State-of-the-Art der wissenschaftlichen Literatur. Zeitschrift für KMU und Entrepreneurship 62(1):57–89
Ordanini A, Miceli L, Pizzetti M, Parasuraman A (2011) Crowd-funding: transforming customers into investors through innovative service platforms. J Serv Manag 22(4):443–471
Pope ND (2010) Crowdfunding microstartups: it's time for the securities and exchange commission to approve a small offering exemption. Univ PA J Bus Law 13(4):101–129
Sannajust A, Roux F, Chaibi A (2014) Crowdfunding in France: a new revolution? J Appl Bus Res 30(6):1919–1928

Schefczyk M (2000) Finanzieren mit Venture Capital: Grundlagen für Investoren, Finanzintermediäre, Unternehmer und Wissenschaftler. Schäffer-Poeschel, Stuttgart

Schramm DM, Carstens J (2014) Startup-Crowdfunding und Crowdinvesting: Ein Guide für Gründer: Mit Kapital aus der Crowd junge Unternehmen online finanzieren. Springer, Wiesbaden

Sohl JE (1999) The early-stage equity market in the USA. Ventur Cap 1(2):101–120

Surowiecki J (2005) The wisdom of crowds. Anchor Books, New York

The Economist (2015, February 14) Crowdfunding: the stars are the limit. The Economist

Wardrop R, Zhang B, Rau R, Gray M (2015) Moving mainstream: the European alternative finance benchmarking report, London. https://www.jbs.cam.ac.uk/wp-content/uploads/2020/08/2015-uk-alternative-finance-benchmarking-report.pdf

Wilson KE, Testoni M (2014) Improving the role of equity crowdfunding in Europe's capital markets. Bruegel Policy Contribution 9

Yallapragada RR, Bhuiyan M (2011) Small business entrepreneurships in the United States. J Appl Bus Res 27(6):117–122

Family Business Across National Borders: Strategies and Processes of Internationalization

Philipp Stieg, Sascha Kraus, Tanja Kirn, and Marco J. Menichetti

Abstract Family businesses (FBs) are increasingly operating internationally; however, they show a different internationalization pattern than non-FBs, since they face unique barriers when it comes to internationalization. To draw a more comprehensive picture of the internationalization process of FBs, we add a financial perspective. We identify the benefits of diversification (with decreasing cost of capital and cost of equity, resulting in an increasing value of the FB) and the real options based on the internationalization process as well as the advantages arising from access to foreign corporate tax systems as key factors for influencing FB internationalization. Furthermore, we elaborate the stages of the internationalization process and observe that exporting and subcontracting are the most used entry modes by FBs, but their probability of opening a subsidiary abroad was half of that of an NFB.

1 Introduction

Family businesses (FBs) are found to be the dominating form of businesses (IFERA 2003), and at least two-thirds of all businesses worldwide can be classified as FBs (Gersick et al. 1997). For a long time, research into FBs was slow to gain traction and accumulate a body of knowledge among researchers, despite the high economic significance (Gedajlovic et al. 2012; Sharma 2004). Compared to the past, this research area is accelerating disproportionately fast in generating and attracting a

P. Stieg · T. Kirn (✉)
University of Liechtenstein, Vaduz, Liechtenstein
e-mail: tanja.kirn@uni.li

S. Kraus
Free University of Bozen-Bolzano, Bolzano, Italy
e-mail: sascha.kraus@unibz.it

M. J. Menichetti
Liechtenstein Business School, University of Liechtenstein, Vaduz, Liechtenstein
e-mail: marco.menichetti@uni.li

P. Droege et al. (eds.), *Cross-Border Life and Work*, Contributions to Management Science, https://doi.org/10.1007/978-3-031-34362-9_6

great deal of research interest during the past few decades (Sharma et al. 2012; Wright and Kellermanns 2011).

FBs are characterized by their long-term stability (Miller et al. 2008) and are constrained in resources and capabilities compared to nonfamily businesses (NFBs) (Jarillo 1989). As a result, their possibilities for growth may be limited (Lu and Beamish 2006). Just like any other form of business, FBs are also facing the challenges of increasing globalization. Owing to globalization, which can be defined as the worldwide diminution of formal trade barriers on industrial goods (Adams 2008), the global exchange in goods, services, labor, and capital has been facilitated. Nevertheless, FBs are also facing increased global competition, and to remain competitive, these companies have to actively approach international markets (Alon 2004). As a result, many companies can no longer confine their activities to only the domestic market. Instead, in order to stay competitive, they have to actively seek international markets (Kelley et al. 2011) for realizing future growth. Therefore, internationalization has become a major growth strategy for FBs. Following the notion that internationalization increases performance (e.g., Daniels and Bracker 1989), FBs are increasingly operating internationally (Koiranen 2002). Surprisingly, very little scholarly attention has been paid to the internationalization of FBs (Kontinen and Ojala 2010b; Mitter et al. 2014), and empirical findings show contradictory results (Claver et al. 2009; Okoroafo and Perryy 2010; Zahra 2003). Research on the internationalization of FBs is a young, but recently growing field of research within the overall area of FB research (Mitter et al. 2014; Pukall and Calabro 2014). Within the last few years, the amount of studies that have been published has been growing exponentially compared to the past (Cesinger et al. 2014).

It is important to note that there is a consensus in FB research that FBs show a different internationalization pattern compared to their NFB counterparts (Bell et al. 2004; Fernández and Nieto 2005; George et al. 2005; Graves and Thomas 2004; Johanson and Vahlne 2009; Oesterle et al. 2013), and it seems evident that FBs face unique barriers when it comes to internationalization (Fernández and Nieto 2005). Therefore, FBs show a more risk-averse pattern than NFBs (Janjuha-Jivraj et al. 2012) and, thus, are less open to growth opportunities in international markets (Hall et al. 2001; Sharma et al. 1997). Accordingly, FBs are commonly seen as slow internationalizers (Pukall and Calabro 2014). They are also associated with a stepwise approach to internationalization in line with the Uppsala stage model (Johanson and Vahlne 1977, 2009) which describes internationalization as an incremental process of smaller steps aimed to reduce risk and uncertainty. However, some recent research (Graves and Thomas 2004; Kontinen and Ojala 2012a) criticizes that such conceptualizations might not consider the large degree of heterogeneity among FBs. Within this same notion, another conceptual approach has been used to describe the internationalization pattern of FBs, taking into account the specific characteristics of FBs (Xi et al. 2015). The concept of socio-emotional wealth (SEW) (Gómez-Mejía et al. 2007) is based on the assumption that decisions in FBs are always driven by the fear of losing control over the own business, and FBs are always aimed to preserve their SEW. In turn, this may result in a lower level of FB internationalization due to their aspiration to preserve SEW (Gomez-Mejia et al. 2010).

The remainder of the paper is organized as follows: the next section gives an overview of the theoretical aspects of family businesses and internationalization. Section 3 sheds light on the factors influencing FB internationalization, whereby the analysis focuses on the benefits of diversification and real options perspective. Section 4 analyzes the internationalization process and outlines the aspects of entry mode, entry speed, and entry timing of FB internationalization strategy. The last section concludes the article and summarizes promising areas for future research.

2 Theoretical Background

2.1 Family Businesses

FBs are mentioned to be the originating form of any business activity (Wakefield 1995) and are dominating the economy of most countries in the world (Astrachan and Shanker 2003; Botero et al. 2015; Heck and Stafford 2001; Morck and Yeung 2003). While two-thirds of all companies can be classified as FBs worldwide (Bobillo et al. 2014), in Europe 70–80% of all enterprises can be classified as a family business (Mandl 2008), and the large majority of them are small and medium-sized enterprises (SMEs) (European Commission 2010). Since only a small number of FBs survive the transition from the second to third generation, the lifetime of a FB is limited (Neubauer and Lank 1998; Paisner 1999; Shanker and Astrachan 1996).

Despite of the economic relevance of FBs, the research dedicated to FBs is relatively young, with the first scholarly work being conducted in the late 1980s (Astrachan and Astrachan 1988; Donckels and Fröhlich 1991). But since then, scholarly publications dedicated to exploration and theory building in FB research have gradually increased (Chua et al. 2003; Pukall and Calabro 2014), and particularly in recent years there has been exponential growth in research studies and conceptual work (Bouncken and Kraus 2013), which makes the research on FB a distinct and established scientific discipline within business research. However, several authors have remarked that particularly in the field of management studies, there is still insufficient attention to the FBs' unique theoretical and practical issues that have been developed thus far (Dyer Jr 2003). Recent research has been aimed at investigating whether FBs really show a different behavior compared to NFBs and, if that is the case, how and why do they act differently (Chrisman and Holt 2016; Gedajlovic et al. 2012; Schulze and Gedajlovic 2010).

In FB research, there is an ongoing debate on a widely accepted definition of a FB (Astrachan and Shanker 2003; Sharma 2004; Sharma et al. 1997; Zahra and Sharma 2004). Researchers usually define a FB by the family's involvement in the business, revealed by the ownership, management, or business succession (Chrisman et al. 2003a). A recent literature review regarding the scientific understanding of FB conducted by Xi et al. (2015) points out that there can be some dimensions identified that have the most research in common, namely, the family's involvement in the business (interpreted predominantly as involvement in ownership as well as governance and/or management), the intention of sustainability over generations, and the distinctive goals and behaviors that result from this involvement and intention (Chua et al. 1999). However, it seems that the definitions do not fail in terms of differentiating a FB from a NFB but do on the fuzzy boundaries in between which lead to a variety in samples used by FB researchers (Westhead and Cowling 1998). For example, in terms of family control definitions that are used, the definitions differ from 100% ownership over the majority of shares until the majority of control (Chua et al. 1999). For some studies, it seems appropriate if the business considers itself as a family business (Westhead and Cowling 1998). Shanker and Astrachan (1996) present another approach and differentiate between a broad and a very close manifestation of family businesses—where in the closer, the family is involved in the daily business, whereas in the broader, the family only sets the strategic direction for the firm. Applying different definitions to the samples of research that has already been conducted in the past, this led to the variation of the share of FB in one sample from 15% to 80% (Westhead et al. 1997). In more recent definitions, another dimension to define a FB was added, namely, the so-called familiness (Kraus et al. 2011). Familiness describes "[…] the idiosyncratic firm level bundle of resources and capabilities resulting from the systems interactions" (Habbershon et al. 2003, p. 451), which forms a distinct source of competitive advantage (Arregle et al. 2007). *Familiness* as the triangulation of family, ownership, and management is what makes the difference between a FB and a NFB and results in differences in structure, behavior, and goals (Chua et al. 2003; Kraus et al. 2011). Moreover, Astrachan et al. (2002, p. 47) stated that a family business is defined by the extent of the family involvement in both management and ownership, because this distinguishes a FB from a NFB, and Kraus et al. (2011) add that the degree of family involvement can vary between 50 and 100%. Thus, when referring to a business as a family business, the owning family holds a significant influence in equity, control, management, as well as decision-making.

Families, as a defining configurationally setup of a FB, may result in a distinct behavior and lead to a risk-averse and conservative behavior (Fernández and Nieto 2005; Naldi et al. 2007) that often is attributed to a FB. Romano et al. (2001) found that the FB's wish for keeping the control and ownership of the business can make a FB reluctant to external investors and also unwilling to hire nonfamily executives (Sirmon and Hitt 2003). Hence, this sacrifice toward external resources (financial as well as knowledge based) results in severe resource constraints (Claver et al. 2009; Muñoz-Bullón and Sánchez-Bueno 2012) and missed investment opportunities (Mishra and McConaughy 1999; Thomsen and Pedersen 2000).

FBs often show a behavior distinct from that of NFBs when it comes to firm strategy and decision-making (Calabrò et al. 2013; Chrisman et al. 2003b). In the past, researchers tried to explain FB behavior using theories adapted from other fields of research, such as agency theory (Jensen and Meckling 1976), stewardship theory (Davis et al. 1997), and particularly the resource-based view (Barney 1991).

More recently, a growing number of researchers describe the unique strategic behavior of FBs by the FBs wishing to preserve nonfinancial utilities (Berrone et al. 2012; De Massis et al. 2014) and, therefore, have incorporated the SEW perspective in their studies (Xi et al. 2015), with SEW now dominating FB research. The SEW concept (Gómez-Mejía et al. 2007) is derived from behavioral theory (Wiseman and Gomez-Mejia 1998), based upon earlier work by Gomez-Mejia et al. (2001), and it incorporates the extent of the family's control and influence on the firm (Zellweger et al. 2012). The behavior model describes a situation in which the decision-maker faces a potential loss of wealth with two possible ways of reacting: one is overall less risky but implies the loss of some SEW endowments, while the other is riskier and avoids the immediate loss of wealth but bears a greater business risk. The model suggests that the decision-maker will opt for the riskier approach to avoid immediate loss. Gomez-Mejia et al. (2001) used this approach to extend the scope of agency theory to emotional and relationship aspects and to show that an aspiration to preserve wealth can lead to executive entrenchment. Thus, they laid the foundation for the SEW concept, which was then further developed by Gómez-Mejía et al. (2007). Furthermore, they reconfirmed empirically the previously described decision dilemma (behavior theory) applied to an FB case: given the choice between a path that implies loss of control over the FB and a path possibly involving reduced performance and a greater probability of bankruptcy, FBs will choose the riskier option in order to preserve SEW.

In an early approach, Gómez-Mejía et al. (2007, p. 106) defined SEW endowments in a FB as "non-financial aspects of the firm that meet the family's affective needs, such as identity, the ability to exercise family influence, and the perpetuation of the family dynasty." These SEW endowments seem to be unique aspects distinguishing FBs from NFBs and may therefore explain their different behaviors (Chrisman et al. 2003a). Although the dimensions of SEW endowments have not yet been empirically proven and shaped (Berrone et al. 2012), numerous FB researchers have been using the SEW concept to explain FB behavior. Family control is one of the key characteristics of FBs, as decision processes often follow more distinct ways than in NFBs (Schulze et al. 2003). Decisions may be taken in a formal or informal way (Nordqvist 2012). Family members influence strategic decisions formally through their position in management or informally through the selection and appointment of board or management team members (Nordqvist 2012; Schulze et al. 2001). Identification of family members with the organization can be understood as the intertwining of the family and the organization that makes FBs unique (Gersick et al. 1997). Further, the organization is often perceived as an extension of the family's nucleus (Berrone et al. 2010; Dyer Jr and Whetten 2006). Both this and the family's reputation characterize the external perception of the organization, and FBs put extra effort into projecting a positive image to suppliers, customers, and other stakeholders (Micelotta and Raynard 2011). If the organization constitutes the legacy of their ancestors, loss would be particularly emotionally devastating for the majority of FB owners (Shepherd et al. 2009). Therefore, SEW preservation thus constitutes the main goal and reference point for strategic decision-making in FBs (Gómez-Mejía et al. 2007).

2.2 Internationalization of FBs

Despite the economic significance of family businesses (Schulze and Gedajlovic 2010), little scholarly attention has paid to the internationalization of family businesses (Kontinen and Ojala 2010a; Mitter et al. 2014), and the current research in the field of family business internationalization shows on one hand numerous important findings and at the same time contradictory and ambiguous results (Claver et al. 2009; Okoroafo and Perryy 2010; Zahra 2003). However, today no clear picture of the internationalization of family businesses could be scientifically confirmed (Zahra 2003). Consequently, there is little comprehensive knowledge of whether and how the internationalization behavior of family businesses differs to nonfamily businesses (Reschke and Kraus 2008). Mensching et al. (2015) conducted an analysis of all existing empirical research, which was published in the area of FB internationalization. They found that five major areas influence research on FB internationalization: (1) internationalization propensity, (2) degree of internationalization, (3) internationalization patterns, (4) market entry strategies, and (5) speed of internationalization.

According to recent studies (Fernández and Nieto 2005; Graves and Thomas 2004), it seems evident that FBs face unique barriers with regard to international activities and thereby only internationalize after having strengthened their position in the domestic market. An understanding of the effects of family characteristics on a firm's international activities that is commonly agreed upon has, however, not evolved in FB research (Fink et al. 2009). In particular, contradictory findings about FB risk profiles seem to hinder a common understanding on this topic. Some researchers pointed out that FBs are less open to growth opportunities in foreign markets due to their risk-averse behavior (Hall et al. 2001; Sharma et al. 1997), while others stated that FBs show more risk-averse patterns than NFBs when it comes to international activities (Janjuha-Jivraj et al. 2012) and are often characterized by risk-taking in entrepreneurial activities (Naldi et al. 2007; Zahra 2005) and resist the demand to reduce foreign investments for the sake of short-term efficiencies. In line with this notion, Pukall and Calabro (2014) conclude from their review of the FB internationalization literature that FBs are mostly viewed by the existing literature as slow to internationalize. Further, Zahra (2003) stated that family members who play an active role in their firm's management are careful about internationalization, even when they are trying to maximize revenue from foreign markets. In terms of market entry, FBs show a broad range of entry strategies (Carr and Bateman 2009). While foreign direct investments were found to not differ from NFBs (Lietke 2006), Mention (2011) found out that FBs with less international experience are more involved in joint ventures than NFBs. Sciascia et al. (2012) prove an inverted U-shaped relationship between family ownership and international intensity. As suggested by Harris et al. (1994), FBs are more likely to choose psychically close countries when going international, which can explain the findings of Zahra (2003), who found that FB's influence is positively associated with the amount of international sales but negatively associated with the number of countries served. Further, Zahra (2003) states that family members, which take an active part in the management of the firm, are careful about internationalization even when they are trying to maximize revenue from foreign markets. Supporting this assumption, Zahra (2003) presents two arguments. First, the long periods of time which are associated with overseas investments may reduce the family's wealth in the short run, and, second, family members are aware of the missing specific skills and knowledge that are required for international business. This, however, somewhat contradicts the findings of James Jr. (1999), who contributes that FBs resist the demand to reduce foreign investments for the sake of short-term efficiencies. Therefore, research regarding the speed of the internationalization process shows a dissimilar picture. While Lin (2012) shows a positive impact of family ownership, Cesinger et al. (2014) point out that especially psychic distance has a decelerating impact on the speed of internationalization.

Concerning triggers of internationalization, Okoroafo (1999) reported that the internationalization process of FBs is a result of passive reaction to unsolicited foreign orders, infrequent monitoring of international markets, and low awareness of governmental supported programs. Another dimension, which has been previously examined as a distinction to NFBs, is the impact of generational change as a trigger on the FB's internationalization process (Stieg et al. 2017). While some studies postulate that succession to the next generation can be seen as a key determinate for internationalization patterns (Graves and Thomas 2008) and is positively associated with the commitment toward and the extent of internationalization (Fernández and Nieto 2005), other studies suggest that FB's internationalization commitment decreases in succeeding generations (Okoroafo 1999).

This may explain that FBs usually take a stepwise approach to internationalization, as proposed by the Uppsala stage model (Johanson and Vahlne 1977, 2009). While involved in international activities, FBs pass along from low-commitment to high-commitment strategies (Game and Apfelthaler 2016), which results in different outcomes or levels of international performance. This predominance of the Uppsala stage model in explaining FB internationalization is rooted in the belief that FBs are usually risk-averse and—as internationalization almost always includes some risk—aim to limit risk by a series of smaller steps with regard to international activity. However, some recent research (Graves and Thomas 2008; Kontinen and Ojala 2012a) suggests that such conceptualizations may underestimate the large degree of heterogeneity among FBs.

3 Financial Factors Influencing FB Internationalization

The internationalization process of FBs can be analyzed according to two perspectives. First, it can be considered as a strategy of risk diversification, whereby the firms benefit by investing in multiple host countries from varying economic cycles and can realize more stable earnings. Second, based on the benefits of taking risks, it can be regarded as real options perspective which focuses on the benefits of international diversification.

3.1 Benefits of International Diversification

In general, there are two motivations for international investments. On one hand, a low correlation between international markets facilitates a reduction of total risk. Low correlation between international markets provides profit opportunities for active investors, and this could lead to a superior risk-adjusted performance. On the other hand, barriers to international investments exist and have to be overcome (Solnik and McLeavey 2009).

From the viewpoint of international corporate finance, cross-border activities and international diversification of production facilities are regarded to lead to a lower company risk because of diversification advantages and as a consequence to lower cost of capital (Buckley and Casson 2010; Madura 2021; Shapiro and Hanouna 2020). Additionally, these internationally active companies will get access to foreign capital markets, which will also lead to a diversification advantage concerning financing alternatives and increase their capital budget (Buckley and Casson 2010; Sercu 2009). Although the optimization of the capital structure for an internationally diversified form could lead to agency problems, from a financial viewpoint, cross-border activities could increase company value (Eiteman et al. 2020). Cross-border activities lead to exchange rate risks, but this, too, cannot be used as an argument to exclude companies from internationalization (Butler 2012; Solnik and McLeavey 2009).

This general knowledge cannot be transferred without any limitations on FBs. Some evidence underlines that internationalization is negatively related to family ownership and positively to corporate ownership (Fernández and Nieto 2005). The question arises why FBs on average do seem to lag behind.

According to Carney (2005), FBs' competitive advantage arises because of their system of corporate governance. With low administrative overhead but by being prudent because of a strong imposed commitment toward stakeholders, FBs probably do not have the necessary resources to start, control, and further improve the internationalization process.

Cost of capital for internationally diversified firms differs from that of domestic companies. The size of the firm and access to international capital markets could lead to lower cost. International diversification could reduce the costs of illiquidity, thus also reducing the cost of capital. Cost of equity for an internationally diversified company could also be lower compared to a domestic firm, as the sensitivity of its stock returns to an internationally diversified stock market will decrease, thus reducing its stock's beta (Madura 2021).

Entrepreneurs and FBs are seriously affected by the cluster risk of their invested wealth. Splitting up this wealth in practice—with respect to the further development of the FB—is often not possible, although legal instruments would exist to make it possible. Because of positive implications of cross-border activities on firm risk, cost of capital, and firm valuation, cross-border activities would lead to a financial improvement of the assets that cannot be broken up for strategic reasons of the family. Thus, cross-border activities can be supposed to have positive implications on family wealth (Bodie et al. 2021).

3.2 Real Options Perspective

The focus of the real options perspective lies on the benefits of international diversification. Those benefits can arise from the internationalization of value chain activities, knowledge transfer, and innovation through internationalization, market relatedness, renewal of dynamic capabilities, as well as differences in national tax systems.

There is a wide acceptance of the strategic importance of integrating suppliers, manufactures, and customers into supply chains to develop new products and processes (Ageron et al. 2013; Golgeci and Ponomarov 2013; Narasimhan and Narayanan 2013; Oke et al. 2013; Roy et al. 2004). Most firms start, develop, and grow within their immediate domestic markets. This implies that initially they integrate domestic suppliers and customers in their supply chains. Such activities include both financial and operational actives. However, the access to international markets often creates the option to generate higher levels of financial and operational efficiency. The internationalization of value chain activities comprises the upstream and downstream integration with suppliers and customers in supply chains. The extent, form, and pattern of the internationalization strategies are determined by three key motives for firms to pursue cross-border production, also known as the OLI paradigm—the ownership-specific advantages (O), the location specific factors (L), and the internationalization advantages (I) (Dunning 2000).

Based on the OLI paradigm, three sets of advantages perceived by enterprises can be analyzed by the value chain internationalization framework (Curci et al. 2013). These three advantages motivate SMEs to hunt for new markets, resources, efficiency, and strategic assets (Dunning 1988, 2000). This framework distinguishes the stages and paths of internationalization that firms follow. The stage is the degree of internationalization in a business resulting from the upstream and downstream integrations of value chain activities. The path on the other hand is the flow of the activities representing that may or may not be representing a similar internationalization stage.

Another question that arises is at which stage FBs, often identical with SMEs, decide to enter into the internationalization process for reaping the advantages of cross-border activities. According to McDougall et al. (1994), when the top management of a firm has previous international experience, productive experiments of efficient resource allocation in a cross-border setup could be beneficial. The willingness to act swiftly in an internationalization process after discovering foreign market opportunities depends on the entrepreneurial orientation of the FB. By entering into cross-border activities, competitive disadvantages in the local market could be reduced to a certain extent (De Clercq et al. 2005). Social networking advantages can help overcome cultural barriers and further promote internationalization process (Di Gregorio et al. 2009). FBs have limited resources and hence they have to optimize their resource usage to make a business profitable. Internationalization through cross-border activities helps the FB to use owned know-how by its business partner on foreign soil. Moreover, it also somehow cancels the scale-size disadvantage that FBs usually have (McGrath and MacMillan 2000). FBs can lower the cost of internationalization by using the readily available internal multinational operations, probable low-cost labor, and technological services offered at the foreign location of the business (Di Gregorio et al. 2009).

3.3 International Taxation Issues

Also, of importance in the field of FBs is the impact of taxation. The internationalization process provides access to a foreign corporation tax system, if a foreign corporation is set up. This generates an option to engage in international tax planning. In general, the aim of international tax planning is to increase after-tax cash flows and the groups' market value by minimizing the tax burden of an international group of companies. In this context, international tax planning impacts the overall corporate strategy of an international investor. Thereby, a taxpayer can follow different strategies. In this context, it is necessary to distinguish between tax evasion and tax planning. Tax evasion is any action by the taxpayer to circumvent taxation by illegal means (e.g., taxpayers do not disclose all relevant information, disclose wrong information, or falsify documents and accounts). Tax evasion is often considered as a criminal act and is prosecuted. Tax planning (or tax avoidance), on the other hand, is characterized by making use of legal rules in order to reduce tax payments. Tax planning opportunities are sometimes explicitly offered by the tax law itself (an example of this would be accelerated depreciation instead of straight-line depreciation) or implicitly offered by legal rules, the choice of the legal form of a foreign investment (permanent establishment or subsidiarity), or financing decisions (equity or debt). In the process of internationalization one of the most important decisions is where to locate a business and, in this context, tax policy is a crucial location factor. Indeed, whereas the effective average tax rate (EATR) affects the firms' location decision, the level of investment is influenced by the effective marginal tax rate (EMTR) (Devereux and Griffith 2003). Devereux and Griffith (1998) provide empirical evidence that high tax rates reduce the probability that a country is chosen as an investment location by multinational companies. As a multinational typically has a parent firm in one country and subsidiaries in one or more foreign countries, differences between countries applying a worldwide and a territorial tax system and the extent of withholding taxes agreed in tax treaties affect the location of the new parent company, whereas countries with high international double taxation attract smaller numbers of parent firms (Huizinga and Voget 2009).

Hebous et al. (2010) observe that the tax response of M&A investments is significantly smaller than choices of greenfield investments. Herger et al. (2016) distinguish between "horizontal" (where firms duplicate roughly the same activities across countries) and "vertical" (which involves firms locating stages of production in different countries) foreign direct investments (FDI). They provide empirical evidence that the tax elasticity of vertical FDI is in general more responsive.

Conditional on choosing to produce abroad, a multinational company (MNC) may have the opportunity to choose where it would like to allocate the taxable income. Of course, this option is limited to the extent to which multinational companies can engage in such profit shifting. One strategy to generate at least some discretion over where taxable income is declared creates the appropriate use of financial policy. This strategy comprises the use of debt and the form and size of income repatriated to the parent company. For example, lending from a subsidiary in a high-tax jurisdiction by a subsidiary in a low-tax jurisdiction generates a tax-deductible income in the high-tax jurisdiction and additional taxable income in the low-tax jurisdiction. Hence, taxable income is shifted from the high-tax jurisdiction to the low-tax jurisdiction. There is a substantial body of research analyzing the impact of taxes on the financing structure of multinational groups. Using data of US MNCs, Desai et al. (2004) find that affiliates located in high-tax countries display higher internal debt than affiliates in low-tax countries. Huizinga et al. (2008) find empirical evidence that tax affects also the capital structure of European MNCs. Buettner et al. (2009) observe that internal debt response is more pronounced to taxes than external debt.

Another strand of literature focuses on the repatriation policy. MNC can engage in a variety of strategies to repatriate investment income from foreign affiliates. In the standard model, the MNC chooses between direct dividend remittances to the parent or real investments in the foreign affiliate (Grubert 1998). Altshuler and Grubert (2003) extend the basic model by strategies, whereas affiliates can invest in passive assets, which the parent can borrow against or which can be used as vehicles for tax-favored repatriations. They observe that the availability of alternative repatriation strategies affects the real investment in the low-tax subsidiary and prevents underinvestment. Desai et al. (2001, 2007) find empirical evidence that dividends from subsidiaries are sensitive to the host country tax rate. However, this finding does not hold for branches. Markle (2016) observes differences in income shifting of companies in residing in territorial and worldwide countries. While territorial countries generally exempt foreign income from domestic tax, worldwide countries tax foreign income at the home country rates. He finds evidence that multinationals subject to territorial tax regimes shift more income than those subject to worldwide tax systems. This difference is however not statistically significant if the multinational can defer repatriation of the shifted income.

4 The Internationalization Process

Since the establishment of the international new ventures (INV) theory, researchers divided the research into two parts, "international at inception" (Oviatt and McDougall 1994) or "international by stage" (Johanson and Vahlne 1977). A boost is provided to the international sales of a family business if and when the family has an active involvement to achieve positive results for the next generations to come (Zahra 2003). But due to traditional values playing a major role, it is possible that FBs choose "international by stage." Direct exporting and subcontracting were observed as the most preferred entry modes by FBs (Wach 2013), but the probability of opening a foreign branch for a FB was half of that of a nonfamily business firm (Daszkiewicz and Wach 2014).

Nevertheless, it can be assumed that most FBs start their first international activities after consolidating their position in domestic markets (Fernández and Nieto 2005; Fernández and Nieto 2006; Graves and Thomas 2006, 2008; Segaro 2012) and usually are associated with export as initial market entry activity (Calabrò et al. 2009; Fink et al. 2009). They may start at an early stage unless they are provoked by circumstances that force them into internationalize (Johanson and Vahlne 1977). Cohen and Levinthal (1990) argued that firms get "locked out" of certain types of knowledge if they don't acquire it early on and that they develop "competency traps," whereby they are limited to the pursuit of a narrow set of opportunities suited to existing competencies. Three levels of commitment are discussed by Guth (2009), which are exporting (low commitment), licensing or joint ventures (medium commitment), and FDIs (foreign direct investments) (high commitment). Hence, FBs show the lowest level of commitment at the entry level.

Therefore, most of the studies conducted on the internationalization patterns of FBs are using an incremental, stepwise model of internationalization as underlying approach (Kontinen and Ojala 2010b). Those results can be explained by the unique characteristics of family businesses, namely, their conservative and risk-averse behavior and the effort to pass the business to the next generation (Fernández and Nieto 2005), as well as their reluctance to change (Kellermanns and Eddleston 2006), which results in a more hesitant attitude to invest in risky projects (Cabrera-Suárez et al. 2001). Furthermore, family businesses are deeply embedded in their community (Gallo and Pont 1996; Gallo and Sveen 1991), and this may also obstruct internationalization and result in different internationalization strategies compared to nonfamily businesses (Mitter et al. 2014). Additionally, Donckels and Fröhlich (1991) found out that the growth of the business is more important for CEOs of nonfamily businesses than for the owner CEO of a family business. In contrast to the family businesses that follow an incremental pathway of internationalization, there are also family businesses that show sudden and rapid internationalization behavior after a long time of being active on domestic market. Those firms are known as born-again globals (Bell et al. 2001, 2003). For the case of family businesses, this rapid internationalization is often related to a generational change or the succession of the business to the next generation as a factor unique for family businesses (Graves and Thomas 2008). Thus, there is evidence in research that due to family specific variables, family businesses do show a different behavior in internationalization than nonfamily businesses do. But the question is: do they do better? According to prior research, family businesses perform better and are based on more solid financial structures compared to nonfamily businesses (Astrachan and Shanker 2003; Heck and Stafford 2001; Sharma 2004), and those findings have been empirically verified in multiple countries (Maury 2006; Rößl et al. 2007). However, there are some studies addressing the differences in the internationalization behavior of family businesses and nonfamily businesses (Basly 2007; Carr and Bateman 2009; Cesinger et al. 2014; Lietke 2006; Reschke and Kraus 2008), but until today insights from a more general perspective are still lacking, and differences between family business and nonfamily businesses remain unclear.

In the refined Uppsala mode of internationalization by Johanson and Vahlne (2009), the authors refine that the primary barrier to internationalization and positive international performance is liability of outsidership, i.e., the lack of market-specific business knowledge. Accordingly, the Uppsala school of thought views organizational knowledge as a particular important resource for competitive advantage and superior international performance. Knowledge resources in the context of internationalization include understanding of internationalization and how to manage international operations to attain superior performance and an international competitive position. However, the firm must possess sufficient stocks of idiosyncratic, rare, and valuable knowledge to translate it into superior international performance (Grant et al. 1988; Kogut and Zander 1993). This seems challenging for family firms that are motivated to preserve the control of the family (Banalieva and Eddleston 2011; Chang and Shim 2015; Gómez-Mejía et al. 2007) and are therefore per se described as owning lower international market knowledge, lower managerial skills, and also lower business experience compared to NFB. Very few firms start internationalization at an early stage, unless they are provoked by circumstances that force them into internationalize (Johanson and Vahlne 1977). Cohen and Levinthal (1990) argued that firms get "locked out" of certain types of knowledge if they don't acquire it early on and that they develop "competency traps" whereby they are limited to the pursuit of a narrow set of opportunities suited to existing competencies.

Particularly, two internal knowledge resources have been found as elementary for international success, namely, education and international business experience. Education is part of the individual human capital and is related to knowledge, skills, problem-solving ability, discipline, motivation, and self-confidence (Cooper et al. 1994). A higher level of education therefore can be useful when making internationalization decisions because it facilitates the analysis of the international environment (Cesinger et al. 2015) and understanding of foreign markets and cultures (Bengtsson and Kock 2000; Gast et al. 2015). Several studies in the extant literature on internationalization have confirmed a positive impact of education on internationalization (Davis and Harveston 2000; Filser et al. 2016; Gnyawali and Park 2009; Lasch et al. 2007; Mitter et al. 2014; Stieg et al. 2017).

International business experience can reduce the level of uncertainty and risk related to foreign market decision-making (Bengtsson and Kock 2014), because individuals can systemize and abstract "international knowledge" regarding the internationalization process and transfer those experiences to different countries (Bouncken et al. 2015). Johanson and Vahlne (2009) propose that the lack of international market knowledge—the liability of outsidership—can be mitigated by network relationships. Family firms can benefit through using their network of relationships by accessing external resources from domestic and international network partner and family outsiders and are, therefore, able to overcome their liability of smallness and the lack of resources (Bengtson et al. 2004; Wright et al. 2005) and also can get access to foreign markets and knowledge resources (Zahra 2005). Moreover, through social networking, the entrepreneur obtains, directly or indirectly, potential partners (Komulainen et al. 2006) that will allow him to start or promote the internationalization process, but otherwise the cost to obtain such contacts is too high (Witt 2004). Not surprisingly, family businesses tend to connect even more with other family firms than other forms of business, and this results in very strong ties in the network of family businesses (Basly 2007; Eddleston et al. 2010; Kontinen and Ojala 2011, 2012b; Pukall and Calabro 2014; Swinth and Vinton 1993). SEW preservation principles of a FB influence the type and speed of learning related to internationalization knowledge (Calabrò et al. 2013). The increase in knowledge resulting from strategic alliances of firms in different countries is really useful to increase the speed of internationalization for family firms (Gallo et al. 2004).

This distinct behavior in the elaboration of networks from FBs can be explained from a SEW perspective, and there is some empirical evidence that has shown SEW also to be valid for explaining FB internationalization behavior (Gomez-Mejia et al. 2010). Gomez-Mejia et al. (2010) found that FBs are less likely than NFBs to diversify internationally due to the FB owners' aspiration to preserve SEW. In this regard, Gomez-Mejia et al. (2010) identified four areas associated with SEW preservation that affect FB internationalization behavior. First, internationalization requires more external funding. Second, the family can exercise more power in a familiar domestic market where they have lots of experience. Third, internationalization requires increased information processing, which may in turn lead to a higher need for external management talent. Lastly, internationalization requires more intensive ties to foreign stakeholders, which makes the family dependent on them. All four of these points may result in a lower level of FB internationalization due to their aspiration to preserve SEW.

The success and failure of FB internationalization process is largely dependent on timing of entry. The research in this area is scarce (Zahra 2003). Autio et al. (2000) discuss the importance of entry timing, because the first international sale is most likely to influence the subsequent internationalization efforts. Powell (2014) observed that firms that are not strong in the domestic markets but have enough resources enter foreign markets more aggressively. Popli and Sinha (2014) argued that financial deregulation really solves the major access problem from domestic to international market and vice-versa. They also suggested that experience, size, and the group of the business have a great impact on timing of cross-border mergers and acquisitions. But Cabrera-Suárez and Olivares-Mesa (2012) show that size matters only in the initial stages and the sector plays a bigger role for deciding the entry time of FBs.

5 Conclusion

Based upon a conclusive literature review, our intention was to illuminate and explain the behavior of FBs in their process of internationalization and to elaborate recent findings on how and why FBs show a different behavior compared to their NFB counterparts. Researchers usually define a FB by the degree of the family's involvement in the business, revealed by the ownership, by management, or by business succession. More recent definitions use the term *familiness*, which describes a distinct source of competitive advantage but also comes along with restraints compared to NFBs. This so-called familiness is also revealed in the internationalization process of FBs. Most studies focused on the internationalization process of FBs have shown that FBs follow an incremental and stepwise process with increasing commitment over the process of internationalization whereas NFBs use more resource-committing internationalization strategies at earlier stages. This can be explained by FB's need to protect their SEW—the fear to lose control over their business results in more risk-averse and more cautious internationalization pattern. To draw a more comprehensive picture of the internationalization process of FBs that is mostly explained by behavioral aspects, we add financial perspectives on internationalization. Factors influencing FB internationalization are on one hand numerous benefits of diversification (with decreasing cost of capital and cost of equity, resulting in an increasing value of the FB) and, on the other hand, real options based on the internationalization process as well as the advantages arising from access to foreign corporate tax systems. We end with an elaboration of the internationalization process of FB proceeds in stages. Exporting and subcontracting were observed as the most used entry modes by FBs, but their probability of opening a subsidiary abroad was half of that of a NFB.

We assume that complexity that arises from international taxation issues also hinders FBs applying more committing internationalization strategies. Instead of incorporating specific know-how by external managers, FBs may rely on building up know-how internally which interferes speed of internationalization. Therefore, we suggest further research on how financial and taxation complexity affects decision-making in the internationalization process of a FB.

References

Adams FG (2008) From Heckscher-Ohlin to the new economic geography. World Econ 9(2):153–174

Ageron B, Lavastre O, Spalanzani A (2013) Innovative supply chain practices: the state of French companies. Supply Chain Manag Int J 18(3):265–276

Alon I (2004) International market selection for a small enterprise: a case study in international entrepreneurship. SAM Adv Manag J 69(1):25–33

Altshuler R, Grubert H (2003) Repatriation taxes, repatriation strategies and multinational financial policy. J Public Econ 87(1):73–107

Arregle JL, Hitt MA, Sirmon DG, Very P (2007) The development of organizational social capital: attributes of family firms. J Manag Stud 44(1):73–95

Astrachan JH, Astrachan BM (1988) Inter-professional collaboration. National Institute of Health, Marietta, GA

Astrachan JH, Shanker MC (2003) Family businesses' contribution to the US economy: a closer look. Fam Bus Rev 16(3):211–219

Astrachan JH, Klein SB, Smyrnios KX (2002) The F-PEC scale of family influence: a proposal for solving the family business definition problem. Fam Bus Rev 15(1):45–58

Autio E, Sapienza HJ, Almeida JG (2000) Effects of age at entry, knowledge intensity, and imitability on international growth. Acad Manag J 43(5):909–924

Banalieva ER, Eddleston KA (2011) Home-region focus and performance of family firms: the role of family vs non-family leaders. J Int Bus Stud 42(8):1060–1072

Barney J (1991) Firm resources and sustained competitive advantage. J Manag 17(1):99–120

Basly S (2007) The internationalization of family SME: an organizational learning and knowledge development perspective. Balt J Manag 2(2):154–180

Bell J, McNaughton R, Young S (2001) 'Born-again global' firms: an extension to the 'born global' phenomenon. J Int Manag 7(3):173–189

Bell J, McNaughton R, Young S, Crick D (2003) Towards an integrative model of small firm internationalisation. J Int Entrep 1(4):339–362

Bell J, Crick D, Young S (2004) Small firm internationalization and business strategy: an exploratory study of 'knowledge-intensive' and 'traditional' manufacturing firms in the UK. Int Small Bus J 22(1):23–56

Bengtson VL, Acock AC, Allen KR, Dilworth-Anderson P, Klein DM (2004) Sourcebook of family theory and research. Sage, Thousand Oaks, CA

Bengtsson M, Kock S (2000) "Coopetition" in business networks—to cooperate and compete simultaneously. Ind Mark Manag 29(5):411–426

Bengtsson M, Kock S (2014) Coopetition—quo vadis? Past accomplishments and future challenges. Ind Mark Manag 43(2):180–188

Berrone P, Cruz C, Gomez-Mejia LR, Larraza-Kintana M (2010) Socioemotional wealth and corporate responses to institutional pressures: do family-controlled firms pollute less? Adm Sci Q 55(1):82–113

Berrone P, Cruz C, Gomez-Mejia LR (2012) Socioemotional wealth in family firms: theoretical dimensions, assessment approaches, and agenda for future research. Fam Bus Rev 25(3):258–279

Bobillo AM, Rodríguez-Sanz JA, Tejerina-Gaite F (2014) Managing resources for economic value creation in the family firm. Eur J Int Manag 8(3):260–278

Bodie Z, Kane A, Marcus AJ, Mohanty P (2021) Investments, 10th edn. McGraw-Hill Education, Boston

Botero IC, Cruz C, Massis AD, Nordqvist M (2015) Family business research in the European context. Eur J Int Manag 9(2):139–159

Bouncken R, Kraus S (2013) Innovation in knowledge-intensive industries: the double-edged sword of coopetition. J Bus Res 66(10):2060–2070

Bouncken R, Clauß T, Fredrich V (2015) Product innovation through coopetition in alliances: singular or plural governance? Ind Mark Manag 53:77–90
Buckley PJ, Casson M (2010) The multinational Enterprise revisited. Palgrave Macmillan, New York
Buettner T, Overesch M, Schreiber U, Wamser G (2009) Taxation and capital structure choice—evidence from a panel of German multinationals. Econ Lett 105(3):309–311
Butler KC (2012) Multinational Finance, 5th edn. Wiley, Hoboken, NJ
Cabrera-Suárez K, Olivares-Mesa A (2012) Family firms' resources and the timing of the export development process. Atl Rev Econ 1(1)
Cabrera-Suárez K, De Saá-Pérez P, García-Almeida D (2001) The succession process from a resource-and knowledge-based view of the family firm. Fam Bus Rev 14(1):37–48
Calabrò A, Mussolino D, Huse M (2009) The role of board of directors in the internationalisation process of small and medium sized family businesses. Int J Glob Small Bus 3(4):393–411
Calabrò A, Torchia M, Pukall T, Mussolino D (2013) The influence of ownership structure and board strategic involvement on international sales: the moderating effect of family involvement. Int Bus Rev 22(3):509–523
Carney M (2005) Corporate governance and competitive advantage in family–controlled firms. Entrep Theory Pract 29(3):249–265
Carr C, Bateman S (2009) International strategy configurations of the world's top family firms. Manag Int Rev 49(6):733–758
Cesinger B, Bouncken R, Fredrich V, Kraus S (2014) The alchemy of family enterprises' internationalisation: dexterous movers or prodigal laggards? Eur J Int Manag 8(6):671–696
Cesinger B, Eggers F, Kraus S, Ambos TC (2015) La heurística de los ejecutivos en la toma de decisiones internacionales. Harvard Deusto Bus Rev 248:34–44
Chang SJ, Shim J (2015) When does transitioning from family to professional management improve firm performance? Strateg Manag J 36(9):1297–1316
Chrisman JJ, Holt DT (2016) Beyond socioemotional wealth: taking another step toward a theory of the family firm. Manag Res 14:279
Chrisman JJ, Chua JH, Sharma P (2003a) Current trends and future directions in family business management studies: toward a theory of the family firm. Coleman White Paper Series 4(1):1–63
Chrisman JJ, Chua JH, Zahra SA (2003b) Creating wealth in family firms through managing resources: comments and extensions. Entrep Theory Pract 27(4):359–365
Chua JH, Chrisman JJ, Sharma P (1999) Defining the family business by behavior. Entrep Theory Pract 23(4):19–39
Chua JH, Chrisman JJ, Steier LP (2003) Extending the theoretical horizons of family business research. Entrep Theory Pract 27(4):331–338
Claver E, Rienda L, Quer D (2009) Family firms' international commitment: the influence of family-related factors. Fam Bus Rev 22(2):125–135
Cohen WM, Levinthal DA (1990) Absorptive capacity: a new perspective on learning and innovation. Adm Sci Q 35:128–152
Cooper AC, Gimeno-Gascon FJ, Woo CY (1994) Initial human and financial capital as predictors of new venture performance. J Bus Ventur 9(5):371–395
Curci R, Yagi N, Mackoy R (2013) Stages and paths of firm internationalization: testing the value chain internationalization framework. J Comp Int Manag 16(1):3–22
Daniels JD, Bracker J (1989) Profit performance: do foreign operations make a difference? Manag Int Rev 29(1):46–56
Daszkiewicz N, Wach K (2014) Motives for going international and entry modes of family firms in Poland. J Int Manag 6(2):5–18
Davis PS, Harveston PD (2000) Internationalization and organizational growth: the impact of internet usage and technology involvement among entrepreneur-led family businesses. Fam Bus Rev 13(2):107–120

Davis JH, Schoorman FD, Donaldson L (1997) Toward a stewardship theory of management. Acad Manag Rev 22(1):20–47
De Clercq D, Sapienza HJ, Crijns H (2005) The internationalization of small and medium-sized firms. Small Bus Econ 24(4):409–419
De Massis A, Kotlar J, Chua JH, Chrisman JJ (2014) Ability and willingness as sufficiency conditions for family-oriented particularistic behavior: implications for theory and empirical studies. J Small Bus Manag 52(2):344–364
Desai MA, Foley CF, Hines JR Jr (2001) Repatriation taxes and dividend distortions. Natl Tax J 54(4):829–852
Desai MA, Foley CF, Hines JR Jr (2004) A multinational perspective on capital structure choice and internal capital markets. J Financ 59(6):2451–2487
Desai MA, Foley CF, Hines JR Jr (2007) Dividend policy inside the multinational firm. Financ Manag 2007:5–26
Devereux MP, Griffith R (1998) Taxes and the location of production: evidence from a panel of US multinationals. J Public Econ 68(3):335–367
Devereux MP, Griffith R (2003) Evaluating tax policy for location decisions. Int Tax Public Financ 10(2):107–126
Di Gregorio D, Musteen M, Thomas DE (2009) Offshore outsourcing as a source of international competitiveness for SMEs. J Int Bus Stud 40(6):969–988
Donckels R, Fröhlich E (1991) Are family businesses really different? European experiences from STRATOS. Fam Bus Rev 4(2):149–160
Dunning JH (1988) The eclectic paradigm of international production: a restatement and some. J Int Bus Stud 19(1):1–31
Dunning JH (2000) The eclectic paradigm as an envelope for economic and business theories of MNE activity. Int Bus Rev 9(2):163–190
Dyer WG Jr (2003) The family: the missing variable in organizational research. Entrep Theory Pract 27(4):401–416
Dyer WG Jr, Whetten DA (2006) Family firms and social responsibility: preliminary evidence from the S&P 500. Entrep Theory Pract 30(6):785–802
Eddleston KA, Chrisman JJ, Steier LP, Chua JH (2010) Governance and trust in family firms: an introduction. Entrep Theory Pract 34(6):1043–1056
Eiteman DK, Stonehill AI, Moffett MH (2020) Fundamentals of multinational finance. Pearson Academic, Boston, MA
European Commission (2010) Internationalisation of European SMEs - final report. Brussels
Fernández Z, Nieto MJ (2005) Internationalization strategy of small and medium-sized family businesses: some influential factors. Fam Bus Rev 18(1):77–89
Fernández Z, Nieto MJ (2006) Impact of ownership on the international involvement of SMEs. J Int Bus Stud 37(3):340–351
Filser M, Brem A, Gast J, Kraus S, Calabrò A (2016) Innovation in family firms—examining the inventory and mapping the path. Int J Innov Manag 20(06):1650054
Fink M, Harms R, Kraus S, Schulz A (2009) Wirkung und Erfolgsbeitrag der Selbstverpflichtung bei nationalen und internationalen Kooperationen junger KMU. Z Betriebswirt 79(1):107–112
Gallo MÁ, Pont CG (1996) Important factors in family business internationalization. Fam Bus Rev 9(1):45–59
Gallo MÁ, Sveen J (1991) Internationalizing the family business: facilitating and restraining factors. Fam Bus Rev 4(2):181–190
Gallo MÁ, Tàpies J, Cappuyns K (2004) Comparison of family and nonfamily business: financial logic and personal preferences. Fam Bus Rev 17(4):303–318
Game R, Apfelthaler G (2016) Attitude and its role in SME internationalisation: why do firms commit to advanced foreign market entry modes? Eur J Int Manag 10(2):221–248
Gast J, Filser M, Gundolf K, Kraus S (2015) Coopetition research: towards a better understanding of past trends and future directions. Int J Entrep Small Bus 24(4):492–521

Gedajlovic E, Carney M, Chrisman JJ, Kellermanns FW (2012) The adolescence of family firm research: taking stock and planning for the future. J Manag 38(4):1010–1037
George G, Wiklund J, Zahra SA (2005) Ownership and the internationalization of small firms. J Manag 31(2):210–233
Gersick K, Davis J, Hampton M, Lansberg I (1997) Generation to generation: life cycles of the family business. Harvard Business School Press, Boston, MA
Gnyawali DR, Park BJ (2009) Co-opetition and technological innovation in small and medium-sized enterprises: a multilevel conceptual model. J Small Bus Manag 47(3):308–330
Golgeci I, Ponomarov SY (2013) Does firm innovativeness enable effective responses to supply chain disruptions? An empirical study. Supply Chain Manag Int J 18(6):604–617
Gomez-Mejia LR, Nunez-Nickel M, Gutierrez I (2001) The role of family ties in agency contracts. Acad Manag J 44(1):81–95
Gómez-Mejía LR, Haynes KT, Núñez-Nickel M, Jacobson KJ, Moyano-Fuentes J (2007) Socioemotional wealth and business risks in family-controlled firms: evidence from Spanish olive oil mills. Adm Sci Q 52(1):106–137
Gomez-Mejia LR, Makri M, Kintana ML (2010) Diversification decisions in family-controlled firms. J Manag Stud 47(2):223–252
Grant RM, Jammine AP, Thomas H (1988) Diversity, diversification, and profitability among British manufacturing companies, 1972–1984. Acad Manag J 31(4):771–801
Graves C, Thomas J (2004) Internationalisation of the family business: a longitudinal perspective. Int J Glob Small Bus 1(1):7–27
Graves C, Thomas J (2006) Internationalization of Australian family businesses: a managerial capabilities perspective. Fam Bus Rev 19(3):207–224
Graves C, Thomas J (2008) Determinants of the internationalization pathways of family firms: an examination of family influence. Fam Bus Rev 21(2):151–167
Grubert H (1998) Taxes and the division of foreign operating income among royalties, interest, dividends and retained earnings. J Public Econ 68(2):269–290
Guth WD (2009) Developing new avenues for growth: challenges presented by five trends in the global environment. J Int Manag 15(3):251–261
Habbershon TG, Williams M, MacMillan IC (2003) A unified systems perspective of family firm performance. J Bus Ventur 18(4):451–465
Hall A, Melin L, Nordqvist M (2001) Entrepreneurship as radical change in the family business: exploring the role of cultural patterns. Fam Bus Rev 14(3):193–208
Harris D, Martinez JI, Ward JL (1994) Is strategy different for the family-owned business? Fam Bus Rev 7(2):159–174
Hebous S, Ruf M, Weichenrieder AJ (2010) The effects of taxation on the location decision of multinational firms: M&A vs. greenfield investments. Natl Tax J 64(3):817–840
Heck RK, Stafford K (2001) The vital institution of family business: economic benefits hidden in plain sight. In: McCann GK, Upton N (eds) Destroying myths and creating value in family business. Stetson University Press, Deland, FL, pp 9–17
Herger N, Kotsogiannis C, McCorriston S (2016) Multiple taxes and alternative forms of FDI: evidence from cross-border acquisitions. Int Tax Public Financ 23(1):82–113
Huizinga H, Voget J (2009) International taxation and the direction and volume of cross-border M&As. J Financ 64(3):1217–1249
Huizinga H, Laeven L, Nicodeme G (2008) Capital structure and international debt shifting. J Financ Econ 88(1):80–118
IFERA (2003) Family businesses dominate. Fam Bus Rev 16(4):235–240
James HS Jr (1999) What can the family contribute to business? Examining contractual relationships. Fam Bus Rev 12(1):61–71
Janjuha-Jivraj S, Martin L, Danko A (2012) Internationalization of a 'born-again global': how a family-led crisis enabled the realization of internationalization opportunities. J Small Bus Entrep 25(2):201–215

Jarillo JC (1989) Entrepreneurship and growth: the strategic use of external resources. J Bus Ventur 4(2):133–147
Jensen MC, Meckling WH (1976) Theory of the firm: managerial behavior, agency costs and ownership structure. J Financ Econ 3(4):305–360
Johanson J, Vahlne J-E (1977) The internationalization process of the firm—a model of knowledge development and increasing foreign market commitments. J Int Bus Stud 8(1):23–32
Johanson J, Vahlne J-E (2009) The Uppsala internationalization process model revisited: from liability of foreignness to liability of outsidership. J Int Bus Stud 40(9):1411–1431
Kellermanns FW, Eddleston KA (2006) Corporate entrepreneurship in family firms: a family perspective. Entrep Theory Pract 30(6):809–830
Kelley D, Bosma N, Amorós JE (2011) Global entrepreneurship monitor 2010 - global report
Kogut B, Zander U (1993) Knowledge of the firm and the evolutionary theory of the multinational corporation. J Int Bus Stud 24(4):625–645
Koiranen M (2002) Over 100 years of age but still entrepreneurially active in business: exploring the values and family characteristics of old Finnish family firms. Fam Bus Rev 15(3):175–187
Komulainen H, Mainela T, Tahtinen J (2006) Social networks in the initiation of a high-tech firm's internationalisation. Int J Entrep Innov Manag 6(6):526–541
Kontinen T, Ojala A (2010a) The internationalization of family businesses: a review of extant research. J Fam Bus Strat 1(2):97–107
Kontinen T, Ojala A (2010b) Internationalization pathways of family SMEs: psychic distance as a focal point. J Small Bus Enterp Dev 17(3):437–454
Kontinen T, Ojala A (2011) Network ties in the international opportunity recognition of family SMEs. Int Bus Rev 20(4):440–453
Kontinen T, Ojala A (2012a) Internationalization pathways among family-owned SMEs. Int Mark Rev 29(5):496–518
Kontinen T, Ojala A (2012b) Social capital in the international operations of family SMEs. J Small Bus Enterp Dev 19(1):39–55
Kraus S, Harms R, Fink M (2011) Family firm research: sketching a research field. Int J Entrep Innov Manag 13(1):32–47
Lasch F, Gundolf K, Kraus S (2007) The impact of unemployment on entrepreneurship: empirical evidence from France. Int J Bus Res 7(2):1–8
Lietke B (2006) RFID-Technologie in der Wertschöpfungskette. WiSt Wirtschaftswissenschaftliches Studium 35(12):690–692
Lin W-T (2012) Family ownership and internationalization processes: internationalization pace, internationalization scope, and internationalization rhythm. Eur Manag J 30(1):47–56
Lu JW, Beamish PW (2006) SME internationalization and performance: growth vs. profitability. J Int Entrep 4(1):27–48
Madura J (2021) International financial management, 10th edn. Cengage, Cincinnati
Mandl I (2008) Overview of family businesses relevant issues. Final report. Retrieved from Vienna
Markle K (2016) A comparison of the tax-motivated income shifting of multinationals in territorial and worldwide countries. Contemp Account Res 33(1):7–43
Maury B (2006) Family ownership and firm performance: empirical evidence from Western European corporations. J Corp Finan 12(2):321–341
McDougall PP, Shane S, Oviatt BM (1994) Explaining the formation of international new ventures: the limits of theories from international business research. J Bus Ventur 9(6):469–487
McGrath RG, MacMillan IC (2000) Assessing technology projects using real options reasoning. Res Technol Manag 43(4):35–49
Mensching H, Cesinger B, Bouncken R (2015) Internationalisierung von Familienunternehmen - Zum aktuellen Forschungsstand in der betriebswirtschaftlichen Forschung. Betriebswirtschaftliche Forschung und Praxis 67(2):76–93
Mention A-L (2011) Co-operation and co-opetition as open innovation practices in the service sector: which influence on innovation novelty? Technovation 31(1):44–53

Micelotta ER, Raynard M (2011) Concealing or revealing the family? Corporate brand identity strategies in family firms. Fam Bus Rev 24(3):197–216
Miller D, Le Breton-Miller I, Scholnick B (2008) Stewardship vs. stagnation: an empirical comparison of small family and non-family businesses. J Manag Stud 45(1):51–78
Mishra CS, McConaughy DL (1999) Founding family control and capital structure: the risk of loss of control and the aversion to debt. Entrep Theory Pract 23(4):53–64
Mitter C, Duller C, Feldbauer-Durstmüller B, Kraus S (2014) Internationalization of family firms: the effect of ownership and governance. Rev Manag Sci 8(1):1–28
Morck R, Yeung B (2003) Agency problems in large family business groups. Entrep Theory Pract 27(4):367–382
Muñoz-Bullón F, Sánchez-Bueno MJ (2012) Do family ties shape the performance consequences of diversification? Evidence from the European Union. J World Bus 47(3):469–477
Naldi L, Nordqvist M, Sjöberg K, Wiklund J (2007) Entrepreneurial orientation, risk taking, and performance in family firms. Fam Bus Rev 20(1):33–47
Narasimhan R, Narayanan S (2013) Perspectives on supply network–enabled innovations. J Supply Chain Manag 49(4):27–42
Neubauer F, Lank AG (1998) The family business: its governance for sustainability. McMillan, London
Nordqvist M (2012) Understanding strategy processes in family firms: exploring the roles of actors and arenas. Int Small Bus J 30(1):24–40
Oesterle M-J, Richta HN, Fisch JH (2013) The influence of ownership structure on internationalization. Int Bus Rev 22(1):187–201
Oke A, Prajogo DI, Jayaram J (2013) Strengthening the innovation chain: the role of internal innovation climate and strategic relationships with supply chain partners. J Supply Chain Manag 49(4):43–58
Okoroafo SC (1999) Internationalization of family businesses: evidence from Northwest Ohio, USA. Fam Bus Rev 12(2):147–158
Okoroafo SC, Perryy M (2010) Generational perspectives of the export behavior of family businesses. Int J Econ Financ 2(3):15–24
Oviatt BM, McDougall PP (1994) Toward a theory of international new ventures. J Int Bus Stud 25(1):45–64
Paisner MB (1999) Sustaining the family business: an insider's guide to managing across generations. Perseus, Reading, MA
Popli M, Sinha AK (2014) Determinants of early movers in cross-border merger and acquisition wave in an emerging market: a study of Indian firms. Asia Pac J Manag 31(4):1075–1099
Powell KS (2014) Profitability and speed of foreign market entry. Manag Int Rev 54(1):31–45
Pukall TJ, Calabro A (2014) The internationalization of family firms: a critical review and integrative model. Fam Bus Rev 27(2):103–125
Reschke CH, Kraus S (2008) Strategisches Management aus evolutionärer Perspektive. WiSt Wirtschaftswissenschaftliches Studium 37(6):335–338
Romano CA, Tanewski GA, Smyrnios KX (2001) Capital structure decision making: a model for family business. J Bus Ventur 16(3):285–310
Rößl D, Fink M, Kraus S (2007) Zwischenbetriebliche Kooperation und Netzwerk. WiSt Wirtschaftswissenschaftliches Studium 36(2):97–99
Roy S, Sivakumar K, Wilkinson IF (2004) Innovation generation in supply chain relationships: a conceptual model and research propositions. J Acad Mark Sci 32(1):61–79
Schulze WS, Gedajlovic ER (2010) Whither family business? J Manag Stud 47(2):191–204
Schulze WS, Lubatkin MH, Dino RN (2001) Altruism, agency, and the competitiveness of family firms. Manag Decis Econ 12(2):99–116
Schulze WS, Lubatkin MH, Dino RN (2003) Exploring the agency consequences of ownership dispersion among the directors of private family firms. Acad Manag J 46(2):179–194
Sciascia S, Mazzola P, Astrachan JH, Pieper TM (2012) The role of family ownership in international entrepreneurship: exploring nonlinear effects. Small Bus Econ 38(1):15–31

Segaro E (2012) Internationalization of family SMEs: the impact of ownership, governance, and top management team. J Manag Gov 16(1):147–169
Sercu P (2009) International finance: theory into practice. Princeton University Press, Princeton, NJ
Shanker MC, Astrachan JH (1996) Myths and realities: family businesses' contribution to the US economy—a framework for assessing family business statistics. Fam Bus Rev 9(2):107–123
Shapiro AC, Hanouna P (2020) Multinational financial management, 9th edn. Wiley, Hoboken, NJ
Sharma P (2004) An overview of the field of family business studies: current status and directions for the future. Fam Bus Rev 17(1):1–36
Sharma P, Chrisman JJ, Chua JH (1997) Strategic management of the family business: past research and future challenges. Fam Bus Rev 10(1):1–35
Sharma P, Chrisman JJ, Gersick KE (2012) 25 years of family business review: reflections on the past and perspectives for the future. Fam Bus Rev 25(1):5–15
Shepherd DA, Wiklund J, Haynie JM (2009) Moving forward: balancing the financial and emotional costs of business failure. J Bus Ventur 24(2):134–148
Sirmon DG, Hitt MA (2003) Managing resources: linking unique resources, management, and wealth creation in family firms. Entrep Theory Pract 27(4):339–358
Solnik BH, McLeavey DW (2009) Global investments, 6th edn. Addison-Wesley Longman, Amsterdam
Stieg P, Hiebl MR, Kraus S, Schüssler F, Sattler S (2017) Born-again globals: generational change and family business internationalisation. Eur J Int Manag 11(5):581–605
Swinth RL, Vinton KL (1993) Do family-owned businesses have a strategic advantage in international joint ventures? Fam Bus Rev 6(1):19–30
Thomsen S, Pedersen T (2000) Ownership structure and economic performance in the largest European companies. Strateg Manag J 21(6):689–705
Wach K (2013) An empirical investigation into the EU policy in favour of business succession among Polish family firms. Horyzonty Polityki 09:107–133
Wakefield M (1995) Antecedents of conflict in family firms: an empirical study. Unpublished doctoral dissertation. University of Nebraska, Lincoln, Nebraska
Westhead P, Cowling M (1998) Family firm research: the need for a methodological rethink. Entrep Theory Pract 23(1):31–56
Westhead P, Cowling M, Storey D (1997) The management and performance of unquoted family companies in the United Kingdom. Centre for Small and Medium Sized Enterprises, Warwick Business School. The University of Warwick, Coventry
Wiseman RM, Gomez-Mejia LR (1998) A behavioral agency model of managerial risk taking. Acad Manag Rev 23(1):133–153
Witt P (2004) Entrepreneurs' networks and the success of start-ups. Entrep Reg Dev 16(5):391–412
Wright M, Kellermanns FW (2011) Family firms: a research agenda and publication guide. J Fam Bus Strat 2(4):187–198
Wright M, Filatotchev I, Hoskisson RE, Peng MW (2005) Strategy research in emerging economies: challenging the conventional wisdom. J Manag Stud 42(1):1–33
Xi JM, Kraus S, Filser M, Kellermanns FW (2015) Mapping the field of family business research: past trends and future directions. Int Entrep Manag J 11(1):113–132
Zahra SA (2003) International expansion of US manufacturing family businesses: the effect of ownership and involvement. J Bus Ventur 18(4):495–512
Zahra SA (2005) Entrepreneurial risk taking in family firms. Fam Bus Rev 18(1):23–40
Zahra SA, Sharma P (2004) Family business research: a strategic reflection. Fam Bus Rev 17(4):331–346
Zellweger TM, Kellermanns FW, Chrisman JJ, Chua JH (2012) Family control and family firm valuation by family CEOs: the importance of intentions for transgenerational control. Organ Sci 23(3):851–868

GPSR Compliance

The European Union's (EU) General Product Safety Regulation (GPSR) is a set of rules that requires consumer products to be safe and our obligations to ensure this.

If you have any concerns about our products, you can contact us on ProductSafety@springernature.com

In case Publisher is established outside the EU, the EU authorized representative is:

Springer Nature Customer Service Center GmbH
Europaplatz 3
69115 Heidelberg, Germany

Batch number: 10726060

Printed by Printforce, the Netherlands